THE MIRROR OF CLEAR MEANING

A COMMENTARY ON THE DZOGCHEN TREASURE TEXT OF NUDEN DORJE

JAMES LOW

Teachings given in Aracena, Seville, Spain in 2016

Published by Simply Being www.simplybeing.co.uk

© James Low, 2021

James Low has asserted his right under the Copyright, Designs and Patents Act 1988 to be identified as the author of this work. All Rights Reserved. No part of this book may be printed, reproduced or utilised in any form or by electronic, mechanical or other means, now known or hereafter invented, including photocopying and recording, or in any information storage retrieval system, without prior permission in writing from the author.

Your support of the author's rights is appreciated.

British Library Cataloguing in Publication Data. A catalogue record for this book is available from the British Library.

ISBN: 978-1739938130

Transcribed by Jo Féat

Edited and prepared by Barbara Terris

Cover design by Alicja Żmigrodzka

Layout by Alicja Żmigrodzka and Divya Gupta

Cover photograph is courtesy of Robbie Terris

A previous commentary on this text is in James Low's book BEING RIGHT HERE (Snow Lion, USA, 2014) ISBN 1559392088.

Marta Pérez-Yarza translated BEING RIGHT HERE into Spanish as AQUÍ Y AHORA (Ediciones Dharma, Spain, 2010) ISBN 978-8496478572

The audio recording in English and Spanish can be listened to at **https://simplybeing.co.uk/audio-records/year/audio2016/commentary-on-the-text-el-espejo-de-significado-claro/**

Excerpts

...One of the things that most children learn quite easily is the joy of spinning; it doesn't cost anything. You just spin round very fast and then you stop and you are off-balance and dizzy. This is the cheapest drug available. You, yourself, make yourself feel funny. If you stop spinning you will be quite grounded, but if you keep spinning you will get dizzy. That is all the Buddha ever said. Spinning is ignorance; just stand still...

...'From one cause many other causes arise.' From the one cause of ignoring the open ground of being, the spacious awareness which includes everything moment by moment and which is a generous hospitality open to everything, can end up as this one particular person with his or her likes and dislikes walking through the big forest on a very narrow path. This is called samsara...

...The focus of our work is tenderness and gentleness and this carries great clarity, because when we are tender towards ourselves we start to understand ourselves...

...If you are out in the country having a nice walk and you see dark clouds blowing towards you and suddenly heavy rain starts to fall, you want to find some refuge. You love flowers, but if you go to a little daisy it won't give you much protection. You see a big oak tree and so you run to the tree and now you feel dry. The oak tree offers protection just by being an oak tree and all you have to do is be where the protection is. You are not making the protection; you put yourself in the way of the protection.

...We usually understand learning as a process of accumulating and building up information, but in this approach the path is about letting go of the unnecessary...

...After a long drive you don't look at the car mirrors to check if they are exhausted. You don't think, 'I will take the mirrors to the

Mirror Hotel for a little rest before our journey home.' The mirror is always working but it never gets tired. This is an example of the mind: the image doesn't tire the mirror, thoughts don't tire the mind.

...Judging ourselves as bad, or lazy, or stupid doesn't help, rather we want to see the patterns of how we get lost. Seeing clearly without evaluative judgement is the path...

...The life of the yogi: sleep when you're tired and eat when you're hungry. It's all very simple...

Content

DAY ONE — 8

- *The how of now* 8
- *We come into being in relation to the world around us* ... 9
- *Confusions arising out of language* ... 14
- *The burden of trying to be in control* ... 16
- *Being there, being in it, being as it* ... 20
- *Here we sit, inside our solid beliefs* ... 23

Why do we meditate? ... 26

- *The first person singular is very hospitable* ... 27
- *Separation from thought* ... 29
- *Not merging into thoughts* ... 31
- *Shamatha practice* ... 34

Approaching the text ... 40

- *Three modes of transmission of the dharma* ... 41
- *Putting yourself in the way of it* ... 42

Lung for Verses 1, 2 and 3 which are about devotion ... 44

- *We hold on to what has already vanished* ... 51
- *Don't trust your map* ... 52
- *Devotion and trust* ... 54
- *Verse 1: The view of dzogchen* ... 57
- *Verse 2: General instructions* ... 65

DAY TWO — 71

- *Verse 3: Meditation about samsara* ... 87
- *Verse 4: The opportunity of this life* ... 92
- *Verse 5: Repugnance for samsara* ... 95
- *Verse 6: Taking refuge* ... 97
- *Verse 7: The commitment of bodhicitta* ... 101
- *Verse 8: Awareness, karma and virtuous action* ... 107
- *Verse 9: The terrifying experience of death* ... 109
- *Verse 10: The living experience of the guru* ... 113

Verse 11 and 12: Buddhahood in our hand 118
Verse 13: Looking for the nature of the mind 122

DAY THREE — 131

Release ourselves from the spell of thought and language 131
Verse 14: The nature of mind 141
Verse 15: The ground of everything 148
Verse 16: The beginning of samsara 154
Verse 17: 'I' and 'me' 160
Verse 18: Recognising the falsity 165
Verse 19: Relax, free of holding 176
Verse 20: Eat the soup 182
Verse 21: Get the point 183
Verse 22: Busy being lost 189
Verse 23: Just a pinball 190

DAY FOUR — 193

Verse 24: The fault of focussing on objects 193
Verse 25: The great completion 197
Verse 26: Abide naturally 199
Verse 27: Confusion resolves itself 201
Verse 28: Always already present 202
Verse 29: Give it a rest 204
Verse 30: The chain of thoughts 209
Verse 31: Illusion and ethics 212
Verse 32: Awareness, awareness, awareness 214
Verse 33: The lie of our lives 217
Verse 34: Be kind to yourself 220
Verse 35: Nothing better than this 224
Verse 36: The proper way 227
Verse 37: Maintain the lineage 228
Verse 38: Teaching for the heart and not the intellect 230
Verses 39 and 40: Colophon 232

Day One

The How of Now

This morning I will say something generally about the nature of dzogchen to prepare us for looking at this important little text. The focus will be on ourselves; on trying to be closer to the basis of our existence. A lot of the time in buddhism we are reading about things which seem quite far away: buddha nature, being enlightened, being reborn in a buddha land, and so on. There is a lot of discussion about going on a journey – going from here to there – and so we study what it's like to be there. But if we are going from here to there, we have to start from here. It is important first of all to focus on what is here before we think about going anywhere else. Maybe here is actually not so bad and so fantasies of somewhere else being better can make it difficult to just be here.

We human beings are always imagining that we can improve things, for example we think democracy is the best political system and so we try to introduce it in other countries. But you cannot give people democracy. Democracy is a particular orientation of the mind which means that you have to start looking at what your initial orientation is and see whether you want to transform it. If you just try to impose one system on top of another, sooner or later, the contradiction between these different ways of understanding the world starts to manifest. There is no magical solution. We have to see how things are and then see how we might work with the particular circumstances.

When President Obama was elected many people were crying in the streets with happiness and hope. When he was replaced by President Trump different people were very happy and hopeful. Hope is important, but when hope blinds us to the actuality of a situation then it is not so useful.

If we take an aspiration like 'May I become a buddha,' we might think that the most important word in that sentence is 'buddha,' but actually it is 'I' because if 'I' am going to be a buddha then I need to know about what is my basis for being a buddha? It is easy to learn all about the buddha and why he has a bump on the top of his head and a little mark between his eyes, but learning about ourselves is more difficult.

Some people go to psychotherapy for years and years to enquire into how the patterns of their existence arose from childhood events. But more important than knowing about yourself, and having a narrative you can tell *about* yourself, is to *be* yourself. What would that mean? To be yourself before you think about who you are. To find yourself at home in yourself, not struggling with yourself or being disappointed in yourself and not hoping to be other than yourself. These are all little side roads you can spend many years travelling down. *'If only I were somebody else, I would be happier.'* But if everybody thinks that then who is the lucky person who is happy as themselves? Maybe nobody. This is tragic because we are who we are.

We come into being in relation to the world around us

I know that for the purposes of fashion many women terrorise their own feet by pushing them into uncomfortable shoes. In the same way, during the process of our development to adapt to the culture of our family, our school, and the nation, we have taken on various distortions and we have become very used to these distortions.

In China, women of high class used to have their feet bound to make their feet very small, but after the communist revolution in the

1940s there was the idea to free women from this practice. However, when women started to take off the bandages that were holding their crushed bones in place, they were screaming in pain because even perverse distortions can come to feel normal and it seems painful, and indeed artificial, to change them.

We have the same when we start to look at ourselves. We have many patterns of identification: views about gender, race, politics and so on. Other people have other identifications. These people are also educated and intelligent which might indicate that our view and their view exist in some kind of conversation, have some kind of relative validity, even though neither is absolutely true.

Whatever we believe about ourselves and about other people has arisen due to causes and circumstances. Maybe you have some old family photographs of grandparents. You look at these photos and you can't imagine how people lived then because our life nowadays is so different, yet their life was their life and that was how it was for them. How it is for us is our life, and it has arisen due to economic and political situations. There are two forces here. One is the notion of our individual agency: 'It is my life; I can live it on my terms; how my life is is up to me'. Nevertheless, we find ourselves making choices from a menu we didn't invent. Maybe we like different kinds of music. We didn't invent the music but when you grow up at a particular period you identify with that kind of music. It becomes your music – the music that expresses your sense of life – through your own process of identification. You give yourself to the object and the object becomes you, and in that way we construct ourselves out of the world around us.

Nowadays, we can see these amazing photographs of the developing foetus inside the mother's body, this energetic meeting between the male and female principles. It has no substance to it. The substance or the resourcing is coming from the mother's body. The baby is growing through taking the resources of the environment and incorporating them. Throughout our lives we are eating, drinking and breathing and without such input from the world around us we would die. We don't have an individual body. Our body is part of the world around us.

I live in a very busy city with polluted air. Last night we were walking through the streets of this lovely town and it's like a paradise as everything is quiet, clean and open and there are stars in the sky. Aracena exists like this all the time, and London is London all the time. When you are embedded in one environment you have the reverberations of the quality of existence around you determining how you can be. In that way we can see that the tension in our body, the way our body can move, the openness of our gaze to greeting other people, whether we have eye contact or not, is something which is developed in relation to the environment.

People smile at each other here and greet each other warmly. If I were on the London Underground embracing people and kissing them on both cheeks I would get into a lot of trouble because there is no permission to do that. What seems normal or natural to me is part of an invisible social contract. In buddhism they call this dependent origination or codependent arising. Whenever we see what we take to be something which seems to exist in itself, what we actually find is its dependence on many other factors; not only for coming into existence, but for its maintenance.

For example, this hotel where we are just now is held in place by there being enough people to rent rooms for the hotel to survive financially. The unemployment levels are high in Spain. When people feel the economy is not doing well, they don't want to spend so much money. When we spend money we are supporting cafes, shoemakers, clothes sellers, and so on.

In London you can see many shops have closed because people are frightened about the economic future, and this fear leads into a retraction, whereby people feel that they have to just take care of themselves. But the government says that if you want to take care of yourself you have to spend your money. It can be difficult to believe what politicians say but of course it's true: we are in an integrated economy kept alive by the flow of money, just as we stay alive by the flow of breath. This indicates our life is dynamic. We are interdependent and our existence is co-emergent with that of everything around us.

Our interactions with others call us into being in particular ways. Each of us has a great potential, but a lot of that potential is hidden from us because of the assumptions we have about who we are, which have been built up in our families, schooling, and our interpersonal difficulties etc. We have become self-protective. Usually as people get older they take fewer risks as they are trying to hang on to what they have. But what do we have? Our existence is performative. If you have a job you are doing your job and showing yourself in particular ways in a particular environment; that is all a job is.

In dzogchen, we are concerned to see this dynamic ever-evolving changing field of experience; to accept that we are already in life and since life is unpredictable we have to find the best way to stay in connection. There are two aspects to this. One is to start from the position that I am an individual and then I can reach out and try to make some kind of connection with someone else. This is a choice. '*I don't have to.*' This is the normal belief system of the modern individual view. But the other view would say that from the very beginning everything is interconnected. You don't have a choice about whether to connect or not, but you have a choice about how you engage in this fact of connectivity. Other people are our lives.

I have two eyes in my head. They are very useful to me. What do I see with my eyes? I see you. I don't see myself. My eyes show me you. You are my world. If I close my eyes I don't have much of a world, but it feels a bit like me. *'Hmm...small and dark and not much happening.'* I open my eyes. Wow! I see all these people. Amazing! The richness of our existence is the other. It is not as if there is self here and other over there; this is a false interpretation - an interpretive narrative - a storyline. The fact is that as soon as you are born as a baby and you open your eyes you start to see something, and that is the baby's world. Gradually, things fall into shape, and the baby starts to swim in the sea of language and to see how words and things in the world have some sort or relationship and what it is finding out all the time is about *its* world. However, what it is told that it is finding out about is *the* world; that there is a world out there which seems to exist whether experienced or not.

This is my first time in Aracena, and because this is a very exclusive kind of place – like a haute couture establishment in Paris where a dress is being made just for me and no-one else will ever wear that dress – I have actually been provided with my own Aracena! Nobody else will have my Aracena, and each of you will have your own Aracena. Here we are like kings and queens because nobody else looks through our eyes; nobody else has the sensations of our body or the patterning of our thoughts, memories and so on.

This is very strange. Each of us has the unique specificity of our own experience and yet we are able to use language to communicate about it as if we were living in the same world and seeing the same things.

Confusions Arising Out of Language

From this point of view, language is like a group hallucination. It is very useful that we can talk about the timing of our programme, about where the toilets are, about what to do in case of a fire and so on since this allows the practical business of living to proceed. And yet each of us finds the world revealed in the particularity of our own life, and that immediacy cannot be communicated. We may notice how gentle the quality of light is at this time of year and how it mirrors the soft greens which are emerging from the earth. Just to walk along the road is to encounter marvels. But when we try to talk about it, what do we say? The words create a parallel universe as the actual phenomenology is beyond appropriation.

When we think that language is talking about things as they are, two confusions arise: we are confused about what we are seeing and encountering, and we are also confused about the nature of language. When we stay within our mother tongue we imagine that there is a one-to-one correlation between a word and the object it's taken to describe. When we see a tree, it's a tree, but when we learn another language we find that they don't use the same words as we do.

This is like a revolution in the mind because the king or the queen of the tree, as tree, is toppled, so now a word like 'tree' is simply a conventional signifier. There are so many languages in the world and each of them will have some way of indicating a 'tree', and yet no one word will be exactly the true means of expressing what this object is. Language is like a dimension similar to watching a science fiction movie, where they go out of the usual three dimensions into time travel and a fifth dimension. It is not that language is good or bad, but it creates a mode of experiencing.

Generally, in the realm of buddhism, language is linked with compassion because it is through language that we meet and try to connect through the use of signs and signifiers. However, there are many other dimensions that we inhabit and in dzogchen, what we are trying to do is to bring clarity; trying not to mix everything together into a big soup but setting out how the different aspects or dimensions of our experience operate together. In order for this to be possible we need space that allows a relaxation, a space that gives each aspect of our existence its freedom to be itself without feeling invaded or abandoned.

If we open to the rich complexity of existence it can sometimes feel overwhelming – like opening Pandora's box – because then we are faced with not being in control. We may want to be more open but our ego structure doesn't cope very well with openness; it wants to know what's going to happen. If we know what's going to happen we can predict and this allows us to maintain the rhythm of our world. But when we open to the fact of many, many aspects arising at the same time, each with their own validity, what does this mean? How will I make sense of it? This is where we see that the ego wants to be the queen in charge of what is happening.

From the buddhist point of view this is the source of our suffering because we set up a polarity: either I am in control or everything is out of control. The middle way is to find ourselves at home in this rich complexity. This freedom arises not from blocking language, but allowing language to take its place and not asking it to do things it can't do.

In your kitchen you probably have many different implements for cooking. You may have non-stick pans that you shouldn't stir with a steel spoon otherwise you scratch the surface. Each situation requires us to attend to its limitations and specificity. As long as you are respectful of the qualities and the limitations of what you are working with they will last a long time and be useful. It is the same with language. We have to use language to communicate, but there are certain experiences that open up when we are not relying on conceptual elaboration.

THE BURDEN OF TRYING TO BE IN CONTROL

In the following days we will be doing some meditation together. Dzogchen meditation is a way of integrating language in its proper function. We don't ask language to do what language can't do. There are functions which we have to ask something else to do, and this is what is called 'mind'. The mind has a clarity to it which the tradition describes as intrinsic: it is not generated out of anything, it is just the given quality of the mind itself.

We don't have much experience of this because we have lived our lives inside the burden of having to make sense of what is going on. Our education is about making use of information and learning techniques which allow us to chop up the world and make sense of what is going on. *'Ah! Now I understand.'* And, of course, because I am making sense of what is going on, 'it's all up to me'. If I stop doing it, I won't know what's going on. Like a little animal in a cage going round and round on a wheel we are turning the wheel of pattern and meaning again and again like a person walking on a high wire without a safety net. *'I have to keep my balance as I need to know what is going on.'* This is quite a burden.

When you see small children going to school with a big bag of books on their backs, this is like the galley slaves who had to row the boats. The children are rowing the boat of their national culture, then as soon as they get a bit older and have a bit of freedom they want to get out of their heads. They feel the weight of a big burden. However, we are old slaves, we are used to this bondage and the skin on our hands is thick from turning these oars year after year. When we were young we were rowing very quickly because we hoped to get somewhere, but now we think we are stuck in an endless ocean but we better keep rowing as there is always more and more to do and to learn. But it never comes to an end. We live within the fantasy that we are going to get somewhere and so there is a huge build up to arriving somewhere at something.

For example, somebody will be elected as the president of America. They will have set out many promises and intentions of what they are going to do, and then life happens; events emerge and the great clarity of their vision is now down in the dust, scrabbling to work out what to do. This is not because they are particularly incompetent, but it is just how life is. The fantasy of control is the fantasy of the individual ego separated from its own ground. Therefore, in the practice we are relaxing and opening to experience the underlying safety net of the integration which is always already there.

The term dzogchen means 'the great completion'. If something is complete you should leave it alone because if you try to do more when something is already complete it will be spoilt. The world doesn't seem complete to us but maybe that's because of how we look at the world. If we can see the natural completion of each moment then the issue is not what to do with it, but rather, here I am as part of this time and place so then moving in the environment, as part of the environment, is responding to the invitation of the field. I don't need a great game plan in my mind. I can trust that life will be enough.

I have to trust that being here with you will provide some words. I don't have any words that are prepared. I look around and I see people's faces and something comes out of my mouth, because it's not all up to me. We are here together creating a mood of communication. Your interest feeds my capacity to share something with you. The fantasy of being an isolated individual would not be helpful to me just now. If I think, *'Oh my god, what do you all think about me?'* then I can feel myself shrink into something very small: *'Perhaps I am doing it wrong.'*

First you make a solid substance, 'me,' and then you can apply an evaluative matrix: good, bad, right, wrong, successful, unsuccessful and so on. But when I am here with you there isn't a 'me' and a 'you'; there is 'me with you'. It is our being with each other that allows the evolution of the shared field of experience and moment by moment it is what it is. This is *dzog pa chen po* – it is complete – it is just this. What else should it be? *'Ah, but James you could have been talking about something else? Why did you choose this when you could have chosen that?'* This has gone and that has never arrived. How you can compare the fantasy future to the vanished past I don't know, but we do it all the time and this is how we persecute ourselves: *'If only I had done that!'* Not possible. Each moment is this.

When you leave this moment and go up in your helicopter hovering in the clear blue sky looking down on everything, you think, *'Ah, now I understand.'* But you can't do very much in a helicopter – you have to come back down to earth. You get out of the helicopter and back into your messy life and now it is not so clear. Helicopter... earth... helicopter...earth...this is how we live. With hindsight we think we understand what we should have done but this is a betrayal because we are extracting ourselves from the lived continuum into a world of ideas.

If you go to Paris you can see the radial pattern of the streets. These long tree-lined avenues have a very grand and unobstructed view, but in order to achieve that they knocked down thousands of medieval houses. The houses were in tangled little streets in all kinds of corners. If you go to Venice, or the old parts of Barcelona, you see the same thing. When human beings live together and get a little bit of money they build a little bit more – in English we say higgledy-piggledy – a kind of organic mess – and that is quite a human, warm and nice place to live.

The people living in streets like that are likely to know the names of their neighbours, but the people living in their bourgeois houses along the grand boulevards probably don't know who is living next door because they have a high wall and a metal gate. This is worldly clarity: good people on the inside of the gated community and bad people on the outside. Inside, everybody has a nice little garden with a perfectly manicured lawn, and seeing their garden we know that they are proper people with proper values.

'I don't need to know them because I already know that they are nice people. They stay in their house, and I stay in my house. Quite possibly, we watch the same things on television. This is a good life.'

It is a completely sanitised picture but our actual life is not like that. Many of my patients come from houses like that. The 'good' man is drinking a bit too much. The wife is kissing the postman. All sorts of things are going on because people feel disappointed and unfulfilled. We have arrived where we struggled to be but it's not enough, there is still some hollowness around the heart. What is missing? *'Oh, perhaps we should go on a cruise. Let's go to Cuba before it gets spoilt by all these Americans going there now.'* Will that be enough? It's like drinking. You drink and you pee, but if you drink and you can't pee then you have to go to hospital.

Our body shows us directly that everything is movement – dynamic and vanishing – and this indicates there is nowhere to arrive in the world.

—But, hang on, doesn't dzogpa chenpo mean complete? Surely if we get to this big completion then we'll be safe.

—But where is it?"

—It's here. In my pocket. Have you not got one?

—I think somebody must have stolen mine as I'm quite sure I had it before!'

It is here, but where is it? Something is not quite right with the way we look. We know how to look for our shoes or our car keys as there is me looking for something. However, this completion is already here, but I don't see it. I see the cars, the trees and the people, but I don't see my mind. I don't see my buddha nature. Maybe it is not there. Maybe I am not ready. Maybe I need to gather the two accumulations of merit and wisdom. Maybe I need to do more offerings and do more prostrations and then in some future life when I am a better person the doors of paradise will open. Maybe I need to have more faith. Perhaps it is not like that. If it is here the issue is to find the way of seeing, which in fact is the way of being, being open to the fact that everything that we experience and everything that we seem to have is, itself, ungraspable.

BEING THERE, BEING IN IT, BEING AS IT

For example, I have a watch. The watch tells me the time. When I put the watch down and I don't look at the watch, do I have a watch? In a legal sense I do because if you steal it I will call the police. The police will ask, *"Well, where was the watch?"* I will say, *'It was on the table.'* Then they will ask me, *"Why didn't you keep it on your wrist?"* and I will tell them, *'Listen, it's still my watch even if I put it on the table.'* But do you have it if you don't even see it? The watch is born for me when I watch the watch, and it dies for me when it's on the table. The idea that it is mine is a legal statement. We have a social convention which says that this is James's watch, but the watch-ness of my watch is only revealed to me when I watch the watch!

This is all very interesting. Even to have children is an idea. When you see them, or cook for them, or do things with them, they reveal themselves. They go to school and you don't know how they are. You don't know if they are polite in the classroom or not. You don't know them – you know a little slice – and you create this image in your mind. Luckily the first time you meet your children they are very small and they don't speak so you can fill them with your projections and they don't object. Later, as they get bigger and start to talk back, it becomes much more difficult. But it is still, *'Oh, my little baby.'* And the teenager says, *'Mum – no – stop!'* The image we have of this child doesn't fit who they are for themselves.

In some way our world is full of ghosts, echoes and memories of how has been, and if we are trying to hold in place the truth of our image about the other then we are a hostage to fortune because life just happens. Our children become people we may hardly recognise and they make their own decisions. Their lives follow patterns we could never have imagined. They bring home the girlfriend. Their eyes are so big. Your brain is going round and round thinking this is not possible – my boy with this girl. *'Oh, mum, she's great.'* How is this possible? It's possible because this is life.

Our children are not held inside the castle of our thoughts, neither are our partners nor our colleagues at work, and nor, of course, are we ourselves. We have ideas about who we are and yet we find ourselves doing other things. How is this possible? We decide to do something and then we go and do something else!

'Who is doing me? I have been taken over! Some coup d'état has occurred! I was only going to drink one glass of wine and now the bottle is empty. Somebody is drinking my wine.'

This is our experience in life: our mental structures and views don't work as a precise description of our interactive becoming. Here we see the essential problem. The image that we build up about ourselves and other people are descriptions of individuals, of some things which can be known, but our actual existence is interactive. If there is a sudden noise outside we turn and look out of the window because our body is good at protecting our lives so we want to know if there is some danger. This kind of reaction happens before you have conceptual thought and this is what keeps you safe if you are skiing or running in the hills. When you are fully present in the activity you can swerve and respond very quickly to avoid stones, or changes in the snow, because you are collaborating with the world as part of the world; you are not attacking it. It is like this when people are learning to windsurf. The wind and the waves are your allies not the enemy. But you can see people struggling on the water because they are fighting and trying to catch the wind. They are not letting the wind flow through their bodies so that they have a delicate harmonic movement.

In this way, we see that although thinking and the use of language is very helpful in certain settings it is not the true solution to all our problems. To windsurf you have to trust your balance. If you are skiing you have to trust the movement of your balance and that you will find a way. Finding a way is not like finding my handkerchief. I know that handkerchiefs are in my pocket, but when you find your way running in the mountains or skiing, the way is unfolding co-created by your participation; it emerges as you give yourself into the situation. You can't know in advance precisely what to do. The key thing is to relax and allow all the skills and experience that you have to flow through you, as you, and to trust that it will be okay.

The founding buddha of our dzogchen lineage is called Samantabhadra, or 'always good'. Good because it's what it is. How to be with how it is? You allow the unfolding of life in which you are part. The basic goodness of existence is revealed when you are a participant and not when you stand apart.

Think of all the judgments which can arise in your mind from some kind of knowledge that you have. For example, if I go for a walk in my local park, which I do from time to time to pay homage to the possibility of exercise, I see all these people running. As I walk slowly looking at the world, my mind is saying that is not a very good way to run as their posture is not good and they are leaning too far forward from the hips. The pleasures of being an observer... This is how our mind is working: good, bad, right, wrong; it is actually alienation. When you participate it's different.

Perspective – the view which opens up with distance – brings a clarity that allows you to see the other as an object and then you offload all your judgements and opinions. Of course, because of this separation you can't change the other. If I were to go up to a runner in the park and tell them, *'I don't think you are running very well. You are leaning too far forward.'* they may turn to me, smile, and say, *'It's so amazing that you, an old fat man, can give me this good advice. Thank you for pointing it out.'* But I don't think so. In fact, the more we see, the less we can say. Life is revealed through being there, being in it, being as it.

HERE WE SIT, INSIDE OUR SOLID BELIEFS

All the buddhist teachings say that suffering begins with ignorance so what is it that we ignore? The immediacy of the non-duality of subject and object. Ignoring the co-emergent actuality we imagine all kinds of things which seem to be separate and to have their own essence and substance. This seems to provide a solid base on which we can stack our opinions, memories and judgements. It gives a seeming solidity to our knowledge which blinds us to the dynamic unfolding and unpredictable nature of our world. The more solid something is, the more difficult it is to change it, as it resists being present in the unfolding moment.

So here we sit inside our solid beliefs and make pronouncements about things. What is it that we sit inside when we sit in this sense of truth and certain knowledge? This is something that Nuden Dorje's text will unfold for us: that what we take to be solid and real is not so. Solid reality is a fantasy of our mind; something is in place and then it's not.

When Spain was inside the frame of General Franco it would have been very difficult to imagine all that has happened after his death. It's like one kind of movie then another movie. I remember the first time I was hitchhiking in Spain. It was in 1967. In the evening when I arrived in small towns everyone was still walking around the square. The smaller towns had communal bakeries where the women took the bread to cook together in the big oven. The beaches were quite empty. The fishermen took their little boats out and back full of fish. Now the beaches are full of people without clothes. How is this possible? You imagine a daughter walking with her mother around the square. *'Mama, I want to get a bikini and show the boys my boobs.'* Would the mother have been happy? No. That time is gone. This was a whole mental world. The proper way to behave with the other people living inside this frame of reference has dissolved like a dream, like a rainbow vanishing in the sky.

A whole new range of sexual freedoms and feminist entitlement has arisen and the culture has become something different. We can see how ideas and beliefs which seemed at one time to be true and reliable are shown simply to be conventions. What was reliable and predictable and gave a sense of shape and form dissolves, and something new arises. We don't know what tomorrow will bring.

How shall we approach this? Nowadays, with computers, people can bring huge amounts of information together very quickly, and many people put their faith in artificial intelligence as providing solutions for the future. But from the buddhist point of view, artificial intelligence is modelled on notions of cognitive pathways developed in human beings. While these cognitive patterns are useful on a relative level, they are actually obscuring the veil that hides from us our own actuality. Therefore, from a buddhist point of view, more and more information creates a fantasy of omniscience and alongside it, a fantasy of omnipotence.

If you look in Wikipedia you can get information about the ancient Greek school of stoic philosophy but that is very different from reading the books and studying and discussing it in a university setting. This kind of 'knowing about' is like a fake tan; it washes off very quickly. If we want living knowledge of the true taste of experience moment by moment we have to move from appropriation and grasping. We have to stop adding more on to ourselves as if we are a vast Lego construction. We have to find a way of naked engagement, of trusting co-emergence and trusting participation, and that is very different from trusting myself as an individual. It is saying 'me with you' gives rise to everything, whereas 'me as me' looking inside just gives me more and more reflections of the same old stuff.

Why do we meditate?

We are going to be doing some meditation but do we actually know why we meditate? We know that when people are addicted to alcohol or cigarettes they feel an inevitability to making use of these substances. People wake up in the morning and they think they need a cigarette. *'I don't feel like me unless I have a cigarette.'* That which is not me makes me feel like me. Somebody who doesn't smoke might thinks that's ridiculous. *'I don't need cigarettes. Why would you need them?'* But when you are relying on and used to cigarettes it feels automatic and necessary to smoke the cigarette. Cigarette smoking has been incorporated as part of your identity; something which is artificial and unnecessary has seemingly become natural and necessary.

When we look at ourselves we all have some addictions, and our principal and most dangerous addiction is our addiction to thought. We rely on thought as the illuminator or guarantor of our sense of self: 'having these thoughts allows me to feel like me'. My thoughts seem to reassure me that I am me. I wouldn't feel like me without my thoughts. That is a very normal experience the consequence of which is that I am going to move towards thoughts which arise in my mind and merge into these thoughts.

If I am talking about a cigarette, there is me and there is the cigarette. I can see that my hand is picking up the packet, taking out the cigarette, putting it in my mouth and lighting it. When I take that first inhalation, me and the cigarette are one. But on the steps to this unification with the cigarette there has been some moment to pause and to consider if I really need it.

With thought it is much more difficult. Thoughts don't come in a packet; you don't have to buy them yet you never run out of them.

Thoughts are available even if you wake in the middle of the night. You are merged with the thought as it arises. Why is this? What is this me who has thoughts? 'I am the thinker' — this is what we like to think. 'I am in charge of my body and I am in charge of my mind.' I think my thoughts. However this is not true because when we meditate all kinds of thoughts arise. Thoughts arrive — we are doing them — but when we merge into the thought, the thought isn't me since there is no essence or substance to me.

THE FIRST PERSON SINGULAR IS VERY HOSPITABLE

The first person singular is very hospitable because it doesn't have any content of its own; it is a hostel not a house. All kinds of thoughts, feelings and sensations arise and are given accommodation. Just imagine all the things you can say: I am happy, I am sad, I feel active, I feel tired, I am hungry, I have had enough. 'I' is willing to say anything about itself. 'I' is the great impersonator. Something arises — that's me! Here I am! I am this... I am that...I am anything...I am nothing...I am depressed... I am hopeful. We say many contradictory things and the reason that we are able to entertain these different conflicting thoughts is because the host is not fussy. I am willing to be anything because I want to live. In English we have an expression, 'Any port in a storm'. Life is very stormy and every thought, feeling and sensation is like a little port. We sail into that port believing 'this is me'.

There are two very important aspects to this. The first aspect is that this is only possible because of the empty nature of 'I'. My sense of being me is full and empty simultaneously. It is full because I am always something — happy or bored or whatever — something is happening. But I can only be filled with this moment's content because 'I' has no fixed content of its own.

Children understand this very well. When they are playing they give themselves over to being the character in their fantasy. They can become a princess or a soldier, whatever they imagine. They see something on the television and they can become like that. They act 'in the manner of' and this is actually how we become human beings. My identity is mimetic, so I am always somebody else but the somebody else that I am, feels like me while I am it. When you are hungry, you are hungry. We know what that feels like; there is some sensation in the stomach and the mind turns towards food. If you are very hungry it may be difficult to concentrate on other things. Small children make it very clear when they are hungry and they start crying. If you take a small child out in a pushchair you have to bring a drink and a snack. They start to cry and you give them something to eat and they stop crying. They were hungry and now they are not hungry. Very unreliable! This is us too. Due to causes and conditions and circumstances we feel like this, and then we feel like that.

This is not a bad thing. The confusion lies in thinking we should be reliable! How wonderful that you can have so many experiences in life. You can be lonely, you can fall in love, you can be despairing and so on, and each of these is true and not true. It is true because it feels true, but it arises due to specific circumstances which will change and then the accompanying feeling will vanish. The reason for exploring our mind in meditation is to see that these thoughts with which I merge and identify are transient potentials, yet I am pulled into them.

If they are a potential activated by my merging and offering myself to them, then maybe I don't have to do that. You go into a shop and there are many things to buy. You could buy many of these things but you only take a few. You see the potential but you don't activate it because you have your shopping list. You look in your basket and you look in your purse to see how much money you have – just enough – so the potential is left on the shelf. In our mind it is more difficult, because as the potential thought arrives we tend to move into it.

SEPARATION FROM THOUGHT

The function of the first kind of meditation we will do is to give us some separation from the thought.

There are two functions of any kind of thought. One is its useful function: the thought connects me out with the world. For example, you might have the thought that you need to check your bank balance. That is a useful thought because you don't want to get into trouble with the bank. The thought is bringing a helpful relationship with the environment; it has served its function. You contact the bank and now you don't need to think about it anymore.

However from the buddhist point of view thoughts have a more invisible and malignant function: they are self-reflexive. In thinking we are affirming ourselves as an existing subject. If I think I am thirsty I need to have a drink. The 'I am thirsty' is acting like a connector between me and the glass of water and this is helpful. But I am also thinking 'I am thirsty', and this is about me. Who am I? I am the one who is thirsty. This is encouraging and reinforcing the idea that there is a continuous subject who can take ownership of the situation, but actually I just find myself being thirsty. Thirstiness arises as a sensation in the mouth and through the identification with the sensation we make the formulation 'I am thirsty.' I am the puppet and thirst is pulling the string. *'No, I am thirsty. I am the master, not the puppet!'*

The more we see that the mind is showing, not making, the more we see that the mastery aspect is an illusion. I become aware that I am starting to feel thirsty. The mind is showing the developing information that creates the image of thirst. It is the emptiness of the subject which allows the hospitality to the thirst. The emptiness of the subject is its value. *'But I am thirsty! I am me! I am not empty. Come on! I exist. You can see me. I am real.'* This is the conflict. The actuality of our existence is the spacious hospitable emptiness. The glue that binds us into an extra urge of identification is the fantasy that I am an enduring real subject.

If you look back to your childhood you can remember different things happening; having a nice holiday in the summer, or riding a bicycle, or having to do your homework. *'I was there. That was my life.'* We can remember all these different stages of our existence. *'I have always been there. Yes, at that time I did look different and I had different interests from now, but in any case that was me.'* So what is that me-ness that seems to exist through time? This is a really fundamental question. The content is changing all the time and yet somehow we have the sense of an enduing me-ness'. *'I have always felt like me.'* But the me-ness of each moment has been arising and vanishing.

The actual state of our continuity is a clarity – the showing of the content – and I can show these different contents because I am empty. But that is very scary for the construct of 'I' which I carry because what is the point of saying that I am empty when I am always full of me. *'I am here. I was here when I woke up. I had breakfast and went out and now I am here. I am always here. I exist.'* Earlier I was outside having a coffee and learning more about this area of Spain. That is not the same as being here now in this room. The contents of that moment – the taste of the coffee in my mouth – looking up at the hillside – hearing an explanation of some of the history of the place, did all happen. I was there but that's not here now. What's here now is *this*, and *this* can only be here because *that* has gone and *I am* still here.

We are now starting to set out the central area of our enquiry into what is the nature of the self. Or to put it another way, what does it mean to be alive? What is life? We see people walking by or we suddenly see a bird and all kinds of feelings arise and pass. This is our lives. When we drove up from Seville last night I saw so many wild flowers in the fields. The light of the sun was very delicate. I am talking about something. I am talking about ghosts. Last night is dead. It is an amazing thing that last night not only died but it buried itself. And it is an amazing kind of burial because there is not a trace left – you can't find a grave anywhere. Even if we had a billion euros we couldn't pay people to find yesterday evening. But let me tell you about my ghost. I was sitting in the car looking out the window and I saw horses in the field. What a nice ghost! You might think I am talking about something, but where is that thing? Yesterday has gone but we can bring it back because we believe in ghosts. We bring ghosts back to life. When a child has a doll, people say, *'Look! This is Mary and she has a very nice dress. Don't you think so, Mary?'* And the doll starts to answer because it is obvious to the child that the doll can speak. Two arms, two legs, one head – of course it can speak. Plastic is not a limit. We are the same. Yesterday has gone and is dead, but we can speak on behalf of yesterday. This is our imagination.

NOT MERGING INTO THOUGHTS

Buddhism says the mind is chief. We create these stories, fantasies and elaborations. In giving ourselves to them, we bring life. There are many creation myths in the world from different cultures. Many of them have this story that god picks up some of the earth and moulds a little person, and then breathes into them and they come alive like Pinocchio. This is a very true story. We breathe life into many things. In fact, we breathe life into everything. It is the clarity and energy of the mind which reveals the world. We are not a thing among things – we are the shimmering field of experience.

In order to awaken to this actual state, we need to not be so addicted to merging in thoughts because it is thought that gives solidity to the seeming thingness of things. In order to do that, we need to give ourselves a defence against the seductive power of thought. Actually, that is not correct; it is not the thought that is the seducer; we are the seducer, we catch the thought, the thought is just walking by. This is the big difference.

In psychology they talk of the locus of control: the site where the decision-making situation seems to be. With the rise of the third phase of feminism there is a new sense of the freedom of women to be themselves. When a beautiful young girl is walking down the street in the summertime, and a man sees her beautiful arse moving, the arse is not doing anything to the man, the man is doing something to the arse. The arse is just bits of meat going up and down. It is the man's mind which is doing something to the object. *'How could I not look at you? You are so beautiful.'* The girl is just wanting to go out. She wants to feel good for herself, her friends and maybe a boyfriend, but she doesn't necessarily want people staring.

My response to you is *my* response to you. This is wonderful because it means your freedom to be you gives me the freedom to know it is my mind. I think you look good. This is my thought linked with some sensation or emotion, but this is *my* experience. It is not about the other, it is about me. The fact that I feel something doesn't mean that I have to do something or intrude on the other person. Nobody is making me do anything. This is *my* stuff – *my* experience – nobody is doing anything to me. Something is there and I like it or I don't like it. This is a great freedom.

Equanimity in buddhism means that we should be equally supportive to all beings whether we call them friends or enemies. I call you friend. I call you an enemy. I call you not so attractive. This is my mind and is the projection of my patterning. When I don't take these arising thoughts and interpretations as being so meaningful, and especially when I see them as being my mind, I don't need to project them onto other people. If I take it as being my experience that is all that is; it is not the truth about the other. In that way, prejudices, judgements and entire edifices of definite knowledge about how people are and what they should and shouldn't be doing, is a mental construct.

Again and again, in all the different schools of buddhism you see attention paid to seeing the difference between the mind itself and the current content of the mind, and also between the current content of the mind and the actual state of what is happening around you. That is to say, rather than seeing or believing that my thoughts tell me the truth about the world – that the world is a fixed thing out there which I can accurately know and on the basis of this can make my judgement – we start to see that the world reveals itself through the quality of our participation. How I stand in relation to the content of my mind is the main determinant of how the world is for me.

We can see this; it is obvious. You walk down the street and you see different people; some people are happy and others are not. Some people have their gaze on the ground and are turned in and others have their shoulders back, gazing out seeing what is around them. Their being in the world with others is manifesting the content of their mind. Rather than trying to manipulate what we see outside ourselves, the key thing is to start to observe ourselves. In order to see our experience more precisely we have to dis-identify from it.

Shamatha Practice

To do this we do the basic shamatha or calming the mind practice, which many of you will know. We adopt a simple focus for our attention. Traditionally we do this by focussing on the sensation of the breath going in and out of the nostrils. We sit in a relaxed way that allows the skeleton to carry our weight leaving the muscles free; the diaphragm, especially, is free. The shoulders are back and relaxed. The chin is slightly down. The eyes are open but not staring, looking down the line of the nose. Our hands are in front of us one on top of the other, and the tongue is turned up onto the hard palette. We gently bring our attention on to the sensation of the breath, and we just stay with that. Thoughts, feelings and sensations arise and we may find that we are being carried away by them. As soon as we become aware of that we very gently bring our attention back to the breath. Guilt and blame are not helpful – simply return back to the breath.

The purpose of doing this practice is to gradually extend our capacity to maintain focussed attention. The reason we use the breath, or sometimes a simple pebble or a painted clay disc, is that we are using objects that are not intrinsically fascinating. There is nothing to think about with the breath.

Usually our attention is drawn towards things which interest us; it's the quality of the object that holds our attention. We go into a bookshop and whilst looking around we are suddenly drawn towards a particular book because something about it interests us. It is as if my capacity to give focussed attention depends on the qualities of the object. In this simple practice we are reversing that idea. This quality and capacity for attention is something that we give to this plain boring object.

Clearly, we have a habit of being more interested in ideas; they have more hooks on them. Like two sides of Velcro our attention and the interesting thought seem to lock together. As soon as we recognise this we relax out of that fixation and focus back on the coming and going of the breath. This is the first step of freedom because as long as the object has the power to grasp us we are its puppets in the world. We walk down the street with all these threads coming out of our heart and we toss these strings out to all the people and things we see pulling us this way and that way. This is how our life is: reactivity. In doing this practice we are starting to cut off these threads and seal the heart so that if we are giving attention we are *giving* it; we are not being pulled into it because this one thing seems very shiny to us.

We will soon take a break for lunch, and I would like to suggest something that you might like to pay attention to during the break.

Generally, becoming a buddhist begins with taking refuge in the buddha, dharma and sangha. This acts as a reorientation away from attachment to the things of this world, but for us as meditators a helpful practice is to pay attention to attachment as it arises.

Moment by moment the world is open in front of us, yet we have selective attention. Our attention is drawn towards familiar features that reassure us about our sense of self. Some people are interested in cars and other people are interested in architecture or in other people, and so on. As you leave this room and walk outside you will be encountering all different shapes and sounds. Without blocking the flow of your experience, just observe how you are drawn towards some things more than others. In this way you can start to see the topology of your own mind; that you have certain tendencies, likes, dislikes, and assumptions, and that these are normal for you. They bring you into a relationship with the kind of world that you know what to do with.

However there are many different worlds. You could imagine, for example, what might be interesting if you were a small bird, e.g. trees, plants, worms, insects... Imagine being a cat that's interested in the bird, or a dog that's interested in the cat that's interested in the bird, that's interested in the insect. We can appreciate how some features of the world rise up for us because we are interested. Another example, in fashion your eyes may be drawn towards the cut and design of fabric but if you are not interested in fashion that is invisible for you. By trying to look through other kinds of eyes we want to open our sense of the rich potential of the world. By doing this we are simultaneously returned to the sense of 'this is *my* world'.

THE FIVE SKANDHAS

Buddhist teachings refer to the five skandhas, or the five constituent parts of the human experience, the patterns whereby we come to have our own specific consciousness.

The first of these is form, i.e. shape and colour. When we look around the room we see shape and colour. We think we see people but we don't see people at all; the eyes don't reveal people. The eyes see shape and colour and in reaction to that we have feeling formations that are positive or negative or neutral. Most of what we see is neutral. When we walk down the street there are many things which don't register at all. Perhaps we see some litter on the ground and we think that's very bad, or we see a little dog and we think that's very cute. We are adding this first qualitative differentiation according to the second aspect: our feeling tone.

The third aspect of these five factors of formation is evaluation. In Tibetan it is *du-shes* (Tib. *'Du-Shes)* which refers to the gathering together of knowledge about something. The second factor, the feeling tone, is like a child eating something and not liking it, and the third factor is the child saying, 'this is horrible'. The feeling tone 'I don't like' is projected into the object, so it is the object which is horrible. This is the way in which we solidify the world and see qualities as pertaining to the object.

But if you are in a family situation you have to say to the child something along these lines:

'Listen, if you don't like it – you don't like it – but it's not horrible. Your brother is eating it so don't insult his food. If you don't like it, that's your opinion and your sense of taste. I'd like you to try to eat it, but in the end I respect your opinion if you don't like it. But the fact that you don't want to eat it isn't telling anything definitive about this piece of food. The food is not horrid, it's just that you do not like it.'

This is very important since this is the basis of prejudice. People sometimes feel a bit uncomfortable if there are too many strangers. They might think if only more people were like them then their life would be easier and then it is an easy leap to the conclusion that all foreign immigrants are spoiling your country. You're entitled to have a feeling tone about whether you enjoy seeing different kinds of people or not, but that feeling tone doesn't tell you anything definite about the qualities of the other.

This movement of objectification gives us the sense that we have access to the truth about the other and this fixity is the basis of all the wars and conflicts in the world. Feeling confident that I know what you are like, and because you are like that, I need to shoot you. This is incredible. The movement from a feeling to a seeming fact makes the world solid and simultaneously makes us very small. Whilst shaping you with my definite opinion, I am also shaping myself. I see other people doing something which I perhaps wouldn't do for whatever reason, and I might decide that is an awful thing they are doing. The more I judge the object the more I abandon myself. I am imprisoned in my definition. *'Horse riding is ridiculous! It's so unnecessary now that we have cars.'* Perhaps hidden inside that statement is that horses are quite big and I am frightened I would fall off a horse. This brings me back to me. Maybe I could learn to ride a horse. If I were to stay with that fear I would be close to my potential and could open myself up to learn something new, but if I just say 'I don't like horses' then there's nothing to be done.

The fourth of these skandhas or organising factors is consolidation, in which we organise our sense of the world and our sense of ourselves and incorporate it with other assumptions. We generalise a conclusion, such as *'This breed of dog is very dangerous. I read in the paper that they bite children.'* We are pulling in bits of information to make our opinion more and more like a solid fact. *'The people in Madrid don't understand anything about life in Seville. How could we expect the government to know what we need?'* In that way people build up these 'givens' whose function is to make us more confident about our opinion.

The fifth aspect is consciousness, in which this sense of the world and sense of ourselves is now operating on automatic pilot as how we see things. The Tibetan word for consciousness is *nam-par she-pa* which means to know formations or 'form knowing'; it means knowing something definite. I can trust how my mind operates because I am dealing with the facts. *'We definitely need to control these dogs because everywhere I go there is dog shit.'* This seems like such a self-evident truth for the individual that they make decisions based on it being a fact. The fact that other people living in the same town or in the same street and maybe in the same family have different ideas is the basis for ignoring them or arguing with them. *'Why would I waste time talking with people like that? I have tried to convince them but they are too stupid to understand.'* However if your idea is right and my idea is right then there are two 'right' views that are very different. If we understand that 'this right' means right for me then it tells me something about the truth of my relation to the world, rather than a truth about the world itself.

This is an example of how buddhism always wants to bring everything back to the mind; it is not about solid things out there. Everything is relational. How we are, our beliefs, our assumptions, our expectations, all of this colours the world as it reveals itself.

Approaching the Text

Now we will start to look at the text. This text comes from Nuden Dorje, the first incarnation of my own teacher, C R Lama. We believe that Nuden Dorje was himself an incarnation of one of the close disciples of Padmasambhava, and that Padmasambhava came directly from the pure heart of Amitabha.

Buddhist texts often include a history of how the text arose, from whom, where and when. To say that a text came directly from Padmasambhava or from the mind of another great teacher, what does this mean? Why should we trust it? Who should we trust? You come here and I am telling you a lot of things. Why should you trust me? If you trust there is a chance you will be cheated, but if you don't trust it's difficult to proceed.

We need to have trust with clarity, and that means we need to be able to look and to see. Dzogchen, in particular, is not about trusting a dogma, nor is it about trusting road signs telling us that paradise is just over the hill in the next valley. Dzogchen is saying that in your own mind you will find everything you need, and so there is a double move between trusting the teaching, and trusting yourself.

I imagine we have all cheated ourselves in various ways during the course of our life. We may have got carried away with some idea and thought it the most important thing but then later we were not so sure. From that experience we may have drawn the conclusion that we cannot trust ourselves. I can't trust me, but maybe I can trust you. But why would I trust you? Who is the one who is trusting you? The one trusting you is me, but I don't trust me! Now I have tied myself up in a knot. This is very difficult. I'm damned if I trust you – and damned if I trust me. Pass the whisky! How have I cheated myself? This is very important. I have believed in things and I have given myself to ideas

THREE MODES OF TRANSMISSION OF THE DHARMA

Many religions begin with a dogma. Christians trust The Word, the logos. 'In the beginning was The Word.' It is different in the buddhist tradition. There are many different registers of the transmission of dharma into the world.

The first is called the 'direct transmission' of the buddha (Tib.. *Gyal Ba dGongs brGyud*) where the buddhas meet together and they don't need to speak or do anything as they immediately understand – it is just there – it's obvious.

The second level is when dharma is shown by particular kinds of symbols displayed sometimes as mudras or gestures made by buddhas. (Tib. *Rig 'Dzin brDa brGyud*) For example, Dorje Chang, the founding buddha of many buddhist lineages has his arms crossed in front of his chest. His crossed arms mean that all dualities such as subject and object, good and bad, are resting in non-duality. However when somebody makes this gesture we don't know what it can mean, because we are not enlightened people.

The third level of the transmission is transmission from human to human, through the ear. (Tib. *Gang Zag sNYan brGyud*) We hear some dharma; it comes in our ear.

I have nice clean water in my glass because it comes from a nice clean jug and, very importantly, the glass had been clean and empty. But when the holy dharma comes into our ears, how clean are your ears? The dharma then comes into our mind. How clear is your mind? We have this question of accepting. *'Well, what you say is all very interesting but I have to think about it.'* Of course this does make some sense, but it also means that we don't really trust the lineage and thereby we are disrespecting the dharma. The expression used for this is 'sitting on the head of the buddha'. You are saying, *'Hmm...I have to check out whether what you say is true or not.'* What we have is a dialectic between clarity and doubt; too much doubt or too much confidence and we don't learn anything. What we want is a state of 'creative not knowing' which allows us to hold a possibility without entering into judgement. It is similar to a scientist who takes something up as a hypothesis: we are not saying it is true but we are also not looking from a distance.

We are going to act 'in the manner of.' By allowing ourselves to flow into what is presented we offer ourselves the greatest possibility of absorbing what is presented, and then we have more evidence whether it is functioning, whether it's actual or not.

PUTTING YOURSELF IN THE WAY OF IT

Devotion is very important in the tradition. Devotion doesn't mean switching off our intelligence; devotion is a way of focussing your intelligence. In relative terms we have to be awake to follow the meditation, so we have to give ourselves over into the ideas and the practice. It is not about becoming a clone, or joining a sect, but of putting yourself in the way of it.

For example, let's say you decide to learn tango. 'I can't dance.' This belief won't help. 'Does the teacher know what they are doing?' This won't help either. 'The music isn't very good.' This won't help. The music starts and the teacher shows. You do what you can and after some time you feel a little bit more at ease. If you stay with your reservations you'll still be sitting by the wall. We learn by getting lost and making mistakes. In the fairy tale the road to grandmother's house is through the forest, and in the forest there is the wolf. If we are going to progress we have to encounter our own fears, anxieties and confusions. These are not obstacles to the path, they are the very path itself! When you merge into your fear or your anxiety or your judgement or your criticism you step out of the music. But then you never learn to dance. We learn to dance by falling over our own feet.

But how do we give ourselves without becoming a slave? By opening up. In the tradition, devotion means that I trust, and 'I trust' means that I am not protecting myself. Maybe you can remember learning to ride a bicycle. When you first get on the bicycle you are wobbling and some bigger person is at hand to help you stabilise the bicycle. Then they say, *'I am going to let go now.'* *'No! I will fall off!'* you squeak but if the big person kept holding the bicycle you'd never learn to get your balance. We have to trust into 'not knowing' because knowing how to ride a bicycle is not something up in your head; it's the whole of you. You find yourself and your balance in riding the bicycle. If you stay with the anxiety then you will surely fall over, but when you trust that you can ride, you give yourself to the bicycle and the bicycle shows you what to do. You find that you are collaborating with the bicycle, with the road, with gravity, and you are learning how to be in the dynamic unfolding of experience.

This is the function of me being here and trying to offer something to you. It is not to burden you with lots of new ideas but rather, hopefully, to convey to you that you can trust yourself and that you can find your way in by trusting that it will be okay. This does involve putting the traditional basis for our ego identity into question.

Lung for Verses 1, 2 and 3
which are about devotion

The text begins with three short verses about devotion. Firstly, I will read them aloud in Tibetan and then I will comment on each of the verses. This is a traditional way of being introduced to a text and is referred to as 'lung' in Tibetan and āgama in Sanskrit.

Verse 1:

'Using this secret instruction one can see one's own face, one's awareness which is the primordially enlightened Samantabhadra. The unitary path of primordial purity of awareness and emptiness spreads as the spontaneous wisdom free of all relative conditions.'

Verse 2:

'Relying on the Guru who shows you the definite meaning, having correctly received the initiations, permissions and instructions, in an isolated place you should initially purify your mind during four or six daily sessions according to the requirements of your own condition.'

Verse 3:

'In this world appearances ceaselessly flow, in this ocean of poison there is no time to seek liberation. We wander again and again in the six realms of samsara and no matter what we try we always experience suffering with no chance of happiness.'

The first verse I read is declaring that I rely on the unfailing refuge who is Padmasambhava. Padmasambhava is the true nature of compassion and we think of compassion as something reaching out to help us. If someone is drowning in the sea you go out and you try to bring them back to the shore. We are wandering in this state of thoughts, feelings and sensations with so much going on, but what is it? Endlessly exploring and enquiring. What is it?

According to the tradition, Padmasambhava is the radiance of the ever-open ground of the buddha mind. Padmasambhava came into the world and displayed many wonderful events, which show that the pure realm (nirvana) and the realm of confusion (samsara) are not fundamentally separated. That is to say, although we may feel that we are a bit lost, we are not lost because we have gone somewhere else; we are lost right here where we are!

This is very strange. One of my teachers, Chatral Sangye Dorje said it is like two brothers lying in bed together. One brother is asleep having a nightmare and the other brother is awake. The brother who is awake wakes his brother up and he wakes up in bed where he is warm and safe. All through the night he was warm and safe but in his nightmare he was not. The actuality is warm and safe but the subjective experience is fear and anxiety. To say that the buddhas have compassion for us can be read in a very dualistic way – that these pure beings who live in a wonderful happy land send some emanation into this fallen domain – or we see that Padmasambhava, for example, is our own mind. –

What is it that persecutes us but our own mind? In my working life as a psychotherapist I have sadly worked with many people who are suicidal and who say they have nothing to live for. Now I can hear a little bird singing outside – this is enough to live for. Imagine if you never heard a bird singing again. I would like to come back tomorrow as maybe the birds will be singing again. *'I don't care. I want to die.'* What is that? That is an idea. Somebody is wrapped into an idea and the idea is wrapped around them, and like in a cocoon they are in the dark.

Before lunch we were doing this practice of observing the breath. Various ideas were coming and going and sometimes we got a bit lost and then we came back. The ideas that caught us and took us somewhere, where are they now? Gone. Imagine that thought that says it's hopeless. You open a bottle of pills and swallow them all with some vodka and you are gone. The idea told me something, but the idea has gone. The idea has no power; it caught you, and then it's gone. However if you give yourself to an idea that's crazy you can kill yourself. Sadly every year many people do that. That's an extreme example but we all give ourselves to stupid ideas. Ideas of regret, like I've wasted my life, or if only I had done this or that. These ideas are like vampires; they keep needing more fresh blood and that is the blood of your belief.

When we look at human history human beings have believed in all kinds of crazy things. At one time there was an idea that you could cure people of schizophrenia by lobotomy. This was very popular and tens of thousands of people had this done to them. Prior to that was insulin therapy where you injected people to put them into a coma, but beforehand they had baths alternately of boiling and ice-cold water. The history of psychiatry is the history of crazy ideas. It was not just the craziness of the patients, it was the craziness of the psychiatrists! People have believed in many strange things even that burning people alive would save their immortal soul.

Therefore, when we are looking at devotion we are not trying to fall into some mad idea that will take us away. When we say, *'Padmasambhava please help me.'* Padmasambhava is the true nature of everybody's mind, the emptiness or openness or radiance of the mind.

'I'm just me. I am doing the best I can. I know I make mistakes but I don't mean to. I am not a bad person – but maybe I am bad. I don't know what to do. I think maybe it's better not to think about these things. I am just going to watch the television.'

We are trapped in this like someone lost in a maze. You turn to the left, you turn to the right, but you can't find your way out. *'I am doing my best, but I don't know what to do.'* And then we start to become small. *'Well, as long as you don't think I am too bad I will just carry on.'* And then we die, and something else happens. We are trapped in a bubble of thought. What is this thought? This thought, all thought, is the radiance of the mind. The light of the mind creates the obscuration through which you don't see it. If you go to see a big waterfall like Niagara Falls, a lot of spray is coming up, and when the wind is blowing and catches the spray you can't see the waterfall. The waterfall is hidden by the spray of the waterfall; it is as if the waterfall is self-obscuring. If on a summer's day you go outside and you look at the sun, you won't be able to look at it for long or you will go blind.

It is the same issue in meditation. If you try to look at your mind as if it were an object, the way of looking obscures it from you. The mind is not hidden by anything else except by our own positioning. This is why in these higher tantric texts and in dzogchen and mahamudra texts they talk a lot about non-duality. Non-duality means not two and not one. It is not that there is really a subject and object which expands out into everything in the world, nor is it that there is just one thing. It is all the mind: the inseparability of appearance and emptiness. The emptiness of the mind and the display, or richness, or generosity, are inseparable.

When we do the practice and we open to Padmasambhava, we see that ideas arise and pass; they have no intrinsic truth of their own. A good actor has to believe in the role so that when we go to the theatre, we think, *'Wow! That was amazing!'* We feel we have had a moment of truth. When we believe in the content of our own mind it has full aesthetic power yet it was only our belief which made it seem true.

Devotion, in terms of the path, means recognising our part in the construction of our world. We give ourselves into the practice in order to find ourselves as we actually are, and not as who we believe ourselves to be. It's not that ideas and memories are the enemy, it is just, as we looked this morning, that they are misused.

Anything can be a bridge or a connection or a bond. For example, when I met my teacher, CR Lama, he had a lot of stomach problems. We were in a small town in India and I used to go on my bicycle to the pharmacy to buy some medicine for his stomach, and through this action I felt a lot of emotion for my teacher. His sickness was a path to my connection with him. Anything can be a path of connection: depression, despair, anxiety; as long as we allow it to be a connection and we don't put in the full stop and make it a firm definition. Nothing is hopeless. No person is helpless unless they decide to be hopeless and helpless.

Devotion means to open the heart to the possibility of awakening in oneself. When we say, 'I trust the buddha', this is not different from saying 'I trust my true nature'. The teaching is our own nature; it is our buddha nature.

We use the symbol or the form of the buddha as a way of connecting with ourselves. Devotion allows us to have humility and, in particular, to really see that I am with life as it happens to me because the heart of the practice is to get into time.

When we think, 'I am the hero. I am ahead of my life and I am going to make it happen the way I want.' We are already projecting ourselves into the future. This means that we are out of time since we don't live in the future. You can be ahead of time or behind time, but the goal is to be in time, time as the emergence, and this means being the shape that fits the moment. Plasticity, not a rigid shape, not dispersed like steam, but ready to take the shape of the moment. I hope you can see now that if you have very strong beliefs about yourself, whether it's believing you are wonderful or believing you are useless, both are obstacles because of their excessive fixity. We are potential and the potential arises as required.

I repeat a story about my teacher in COLLECTED WORKS OF CR LAMA When he was young he had been recognised as a tulku, an incarnation, and he was given a throne to sit on. When they had big ceremonies local people would come and offer some scarves, and because there were many other lamas in the monastery my teacher didn't always get a scarf. If somebody was not going to offer him a scarf but he leant forward as if to receive one then this was very bad form, however if somebody was offering a scarf and he didn't lean forward to receive it then this was also very bad. His tutor was sitting beside him and would lean across and whack him on the back of the head. This whack was telling him not to sit in his thoughts; not to be in his own idea about may or may not happen. If you are here in the moment, as soon as the other person starts to move, then you are right there. This is to be in the rhythm of life.

Maybe some of you know this wonderful film "The Seven Samurai" from Akira Kurosawa? I think this is a brilliant film because it's the study of anxiety and how anxiety sabotages timing. When you are anxious you either run ahead or you are too late. Again and again the master samurai is just on the point. He has great compassion. He says, *'You don't want to fight with me, do you?'* But then this poor idiot is dead because he was in his anger and egotism. He didn't see that the other man was just waiting, was in time ion the situation, that his life was moving like a wave.

The meditation texts say that when you are sitting in meditation don't go after past thoughts and don't wait expectantly for future thoughts, like a cat outside a mouse hole. Be here. Whatever is, is. What gets in the way of our doing that is opinion and judgement. One thought arises... it's going by... stupid thought! The next thought has stabbed us through the heart. Why were we looking back? The thought is gone but we wanted to stick our little judgement on to it. What for? Because we need to say to the world what it is.

The function of the ego is commentarial: it has always got something to say such as good, bad, right, wrong, I like or I don't like, or this shouldn't happen. There is no end and it's out of time as the commentary comes after the fact. In England we have a children's game where you have a big drawing of a donkey. Children are blindfolded and they are given a little tail which they have to pin or to the donkey. They are trying to work out where it should go. Whilst we give our wonderful wise judgements about life, the donkey has already gone. What do we think about these presidential candidates in America? We look in the pocket and we have many donkey tails: good, bad, stupid, mad, wonderful. But where is the donkey? A thousand tails and no donkey. It's gone. It is in America, or it is in the past, or in the future.

This is the meaning of samsara. Samsara is the flow of thoughts, of mental constructions of ideas about something else which is the richness and creativity of our own mind. This is the reason we are stupid. We are stupid because of our own creativity. Wow! That's amazing. It is not as if there is some demon or devil or obstacle out there doing this to us; it's that we don't recognise that an idea is an idea. We have had billions of ideas since we were born. Have any of these ideas stayed? The idea lasts less than a second. *'I'm hot. I'm cold. I'm tired.'* It vanishes and yet we have built these huge structures on top of empty ideas.

Therefore, the difference between samsara and nirvana is that in nirvana we say a thought is a thought, and in samsara we say a thought is a fact, that it is solid, real and reliable, despite that it's gone. This is ignoring the nature of thought. This is the delusion of believing that something which is manifestly impermanent is actually permanent. It is important to acknowledge and observe how we do this.

WE HOLD ON TO WHAT HAS ALREADY VANISHED

Since we woke up this morning we have had many thoughts and all of them have vanished because this is what thoughts do. They are like little gestures that move us around. They have an impact. They are like the music of life but you can't hold on to music. Music reveals itself in its vanishing and thoughts also reveal themselves in their vanishing. When we grasp at something, what do we get? We get a sequence of ideas which seem to indicate something.

For example, on a dark summer's night if you have a fire outside and you take a stick out of the fire, the end of the stick glows and if you turn it around your head you make a circle of fire. There is no actual circle. This is an illusion created by the speed of turning the stick. You see something which is not really there – like a mirage – like a rainbow – like the reflection of the moon on water. These are traditional buddhist examples of illusion. The flow of our thoughts creates the illusion that there are substantial entities, but each of these thoughts is a momentary expression of the vitality of the mind.

This world is like a vast collection of snakeskins. Every year the snake is sloughing off its old skin leaving an echo shape of what it was. The life of the snake has moved on, but the skin of the snake remains and this is what we hold on to.

I am a lucky person since I had a very good mother and I loved my mother very much and I could tell you many stories about my mother, but actually my mother is dead. I was there at the crematorium service when they burnt her. *'What kind of son am I to let them burn my mother?!'* I took her ashes and I put them in the sea all around Britain, and threw them on the mountains. I took some of the ashes to a seaside town where we had enjoyed the best ice cream in Scotland. This is the cult of the ghost. When I took the ashes and I put them in the sea, I felt a lot of emotion with tears coming out of my eyes. *'Oh, I love this ghost.'* Where was my mother? Somewhere... gone... but I love her. This is our mind. In these moments we can see how we put the meaning into something. This is a construction of the mind. There is nothing wrong with it but it's not real because there is nothing real.

In European thinking, reality is polarised with fantasy If something is not real t must be a fantasy. If you go to Disneyland, for the children it is real, but for the parents it's a very expensive fantasy!

Don't trust your map

In the buddhist tradition they don't use this polarity. This word 'real' from the Latin 'res' means thing: a substance which has an internal defining essence, but from the buddhist point of view there is no essence.

Essence is a mental projection. We are in a town called Aracena, but it doesn't exist. There are many streets in Aracena. Are we in the best part of Aracena? Maybe there are some parts of Aracena which are more Aracena than this part, so where is the Aracena of Aracena? This will depend on the person. The person who lives here may say it's their house, or if somebody is a Catholic they will maybe say the church or the old castle. These are all possibilities which are taken up by our mind according to our historical formations. That is to say Aracena is co-emergent with our presence; there is no Aracena without you and you will only ever get your own Aracena. This is very strange because we think Aracena is here. You can look at the map and the streets and you can learn about its history, therefore, it exists. Okay, it exists, but what does it exist as? Streets, cars, people, cafes. How do you know they are there? Well, I look at the map. Maybe it has changed since the map was drawn. I was on the street this morning and I remember what it was like.

If I walked down the street again I might see a car that wasn't there this morning. *'That doesn't matter. The street is there. Whether that car is there or not it is still the same street.'* In the morning the sky was blue, the light was clear, and the colour of the white houses was vivid. This afternoon there are clouds, and the light is muted, so the street looks different. *'It doesn't matter what the street looks like, it's the same street.'* Is this true? *'Listen, look at the street name; it was the same this morning so it's the same street. The name guarantees the product.'* But it doesn't look the same. *'Don't worry about how it looks, essentially, it is the same.'* So what is the essence of the street? *'It's the shape of the houses.'* But the shape of the houses looks different with the change of the light. *'No, but the real shape of the houses hasn't changed since this morning.'* But in your experience it has and this is fundamental. There is a map and there is a territory and the territory keeps changing. This is confusing but luckily for us we have a map and the map doesn't change.

'Aracena is Aracena. I have lived here all my life. I went to school here and I can tell you it's the same town. Well, a few things have changed. The police station has moved and some of the roads have been widened, and this market place has been changed a bit. Some new buildings are here. Some of the old people have died and new people have arrived. Despite all of that, Aracena is Aracena.'

To see that the world is changing is quite shocking because you then realise that you are talking rubbish because you are talking as if it were always the same.

'But I'm just me, I have always been me, even when I was inside my mother's belly I was me.'

This is where we see the seduction embedded in belief in the idea. Trust in ideas is our way of avoiding phenomenology. If we are practising any kind of buddhism then in the beginning we think about impermanence. Impermanence is a way of saying don't trust your map; try to stay with the territory even though the territory is always changing. That is what is meant when we talk about focussed attention and awareness – being here in the moment as the world changes, not sitting inside your map. Maps are always out of date anyway and that means we each have to make our own map moment by moment.

The meditation practice is designed to help us move from being a map reader to a map maker, but this map that we are making is a particular map and a particular take on things. If we want our map to be up-to-date, actual and connected then we have to be here. This is what being awake means in buddhism.

DEVOTION AND TRUST

Devotion means 'I need help'. I open myself to the buddhas because I am a mere map reader. When we act impulsively we are taking an old pattern and bringing it into a new situation.

This is different from being spontaneous and improvising because when you improvise you are working in the freshness of the moment, but when you run an impulse you are running a previously established pattern of behaviour. For example, a few years ago I was in San Sebastian. It was a wonderful weekend because a festival was happening and there were many activities with various groups dancing and singing. There was one group who were doing movement improvisation, and they had a couple of guys playing guitar with some very nice spontaneous music and about a dozen people were moving around on a big carpeted area. The idea was that with each movement people would come into contact with someone else and respond to that, allowing the inter-movement to create new forms. What quickly became apparent was that there were only two people who could really improvise because the other people all had a limited repertoire of moves they could make, and they would repeat these again and again. There is nothing wrong with that, but what they were doing was taking the past into the present; they weren't allowing the fresh new situation to make them fresh. You could see in the hesitancy, the anxiety of not knowing what to do next, and of course this is disastrous because now you go into your conceptual system to try to tell you what to do. But there isn't anything to do except move into the situation.

The meaning of devotion is that again and again we trust that the moment is enough; not underprepared or over prepared, but available. This makes us very soft because we start to trust. Some of you may have devotional practices like praying to Tara, and these are very useful because it's a way of allowing ourselves to be in communication and through that we find some space of freshness. We are our own limit.

As adults we might have difficult relationships or problems at work; there are certain limiting factors which we have to manage but essentially we are our own real limit – what we believe about ourselves and what we say to ourselves. That's why the key or basis of the practice is to observe ourselves. How do I think about myself? How do I think about other people? When I have a feeling, can I be with my feeling? If I am sad or lonely can I allow myself to be with that? Not entering into judgement about it but 'tasting' loneliness, sadness, failure or disappointment. We might say these are too bitter, but a bitter taste is also useful in cooking. Bitter is a recognised taste. *'But I don't like it. I want something sweet.'* But you don't have sweet, you have bitter. What is bitter? Taste it. *'I've messed up. How did I end up here?'*

For meditators this is very important. This is a taste and if you open to that taste it will kiss you and leave you as thoughts always do – they are here and gone – it won't catch you forever. If you try and resist the bitterness it will wrap itself around you. This is what Freudians call the return of the repressed because whenever you try to manipulate and control your mind its own life energy will bubble up again. What this is pointing towards is generosity and hospitality without judgement. We can feel, 'I am jealous,' or 'I am filled with longings that will never be fulfilled.' What is this like? You feel hollow, empty, hot or cold, shaky – it is just this – and then it's gone.

If you can inhabit your own existence without blaming yourself, what a beautiful basis for compassion. If you hate yourself, how will you ever help anyone else? Self-acceptance – being with the mind as it is – is truly the basis for connection. Allowing the mind to be as it is. To experience everything which arises and see that it is always impermanent. In the dzogchen tradition this is referred to as the self-liberation of the mind.

Let's say you have a feeling, *'I hate myself, I am so stupid.'* Without merging into the thought and without trying to push it away, just give it hospitality. It is there and then it's gone, because it always does go. No thought, sensation or emotion ever remains. Spending a lot of energy trying to get rid of something which will go by itself is foolish, especially since, paradoxically, it reinforces the seeming solidity of the thought.

It is very important just to allow ourselves to be as we are. *'But if other people see I am sad, what will they think?'* They will think whatever they think. Freedom for you to have your thoughts and freedom. For me to be me is better than pretending.

Verse 1: The View of Dzogchen

"Using this secret instruction one can see one's own face, one's awareness which is the primordially enlightened Samantabhadra. The unity path of primordial purity of awareness and emptiness spreads as the spontaneous wisdom free of all relative conditions."

Nuden Dorje is saying this is a text to help one see one's own face. Our own face is something we have always had but we have never seen. We have seen photographs or reflections but we can't see our own face directly. You can, however, be your face. To be fully alive and inhabiting your own existence is the meaning of seeing your own face. You don't see it as an object but it radiates from you as part of your being in the world. This face is one's own awareness which is not other than the original Buddha, or the primordially enlightened Samantabhadra.

'Awareness' in this text doesn't refer to dualistic consciousness. With your consciousness you can know things **about** your face. You see your face in the mirror and you build up some mental images of how you look. This is yourself as a subject having ideas about how you are. By awareness is meant the immediate presence of what is occurring.

We may sometimes have that experience in nature – being out in the hills, watching the sunset is beautiful and peaceful. A lot is happening but there is nothing really to think about. We find ourselves just being present with what is occurring, that is to say the mind is receiving the gift of life. We have a holiday from the endless busyness with which we are engaged, telling the world what it is and telling ourselves who we are – narratives of explanation and commentary. But with the sunset you are just there as it is happening to you, for you, and with you. You are getting everything, yet you are not getting anything.

This is the particular quality of awareness and this is why awareness is always fresh. If you get some-thing then you have to store it some-place. Our consciousness is always storing bits of memory and information and building up pictures, but awareness effortlessly allows everything to go. It has no need to cling because there is no basis for clinging. We will return to this point many times.

As an individual, as an ego, I think we all experience some sense of loss or lack. Our life is not quite perfect or complete. There are changes we would like to make – things to get rid of and things to get more of. When we find ourselves in that state this is an indication that it is our ego functioning. Not a bad thing, it is just how it is.

This is not the same as awareness. Awareness is the generous hospitality of the mind which takes hold of nothing. Awareness is not something which has any lack; it doesn't need something more nor does it have an excess and need to get rid of something. Awareness fills and empties with the flow of the world. As we looked earlier today, this is like the first person singular. 'I' is in fact the site or the point of our awareness since it is empty and always filling. However, there is a kind of spin in this, of feeling that something has to be done, of wanting to hang onto things we like or getting rid of things we don't like. Let's say, for example, that we feel sad. There is the feeling of sadness and then there is the commentary, 'I don't like being sad. I wish I wasn't sad. Why do I have to be sad? Other people are luckier than me.' Many different thoughts can arise around this and that activity of the engagement of associative thoughts blocks the simplicity of just being sad. If we are simply sad, we are sad for a while, and then it goes.

This has a great implication for meditation since it means whatever arises in the mind **shows** the mind, so if you want to find your mind just be with whatever is occurring. The mind is not going to be indicated by something special or extraordinary; it is indicated by whatever is occurring. Feeling hungry, feeling happy, feeling sad, are each a door to the mind itself. These experiences arise because there is a knower. Life is experienced and it is revealed; it is shown, it is known. When you layer a veil of interpretation over it, thinking that your interpretation adds meaning and value, then you get further and further away from the thing itself.

WINE TASTING: HOW COMPARING AND CONTRASTING INCREASES OUR CONFUSION

Let's say you are going to have a glass of wine. You open the bottle and pour it into the glass. You hear this marvellous sound... glug... glug ...glug. This is the sign of a full bottle. A royal road of happiness lies ahead of you! You swirl the wine around in the glass. You see the colour and the viscosity and whether it has legs coming down on the glass or not. You smell it and you take a first sip. This is the wine, but then you start to talk about the wine. Everything you say about the wine takes you further from the wine because now you are tasting it with the idea, and this is like an anaesthetic on your tongue. *'Ah, yes, it's a little bit like that bottle of wine I had last week.'* Is the 'live' wine in the glass being improved by comparing it to a 'dead' glass of wine from last week? *'It is not quite as good as that one. Where is that wine? Hey, I'll have a bottle of that. I'd like to get you one from the cellar but how do I get into a week ago?'* What you have is what you have. What is it?

When you start to talk **about** something, you are pulled into comparing and contrasting what is here with something which is elsewhere. The only way to do that is to make what is here the same as what is there, but 'what is there' is an idea, and 'what is here' is wine in the glass; so we transform the wine in the glass to an **idea** about the wine in the glass. I successfully compare the idea of this wine with the idea of that wine. This is how a great deal of our mental space is occupied with echoes of echoes. The immediacy of the taste is gone because when you smell the wine, what can you really say? *'Hmm... something of autumn... blackcurrant...'* You are comparing and contrasting. It doesn't taste like blackcurrants, it tastes like wine. What it is like is not what it is, and what it is you can't say. So just drink it and enjoy! But we have to talk, we have to have culture – in this way we create a buffer zone between ourselves and the world. We have the possibility of direct experience but then it gets mediated through our ideas.

Therefore, when Nuden Dorje is saying **'see your own face'** this means immediate unmediated experience – not interpreted, not added to by something else but just this. Because this won't last very long. Something else will happen.

In the realm of psychoanalysis is what is called 'object relations theory'. This describes how a child starts to build up images in its mind about significant people surrounding them, so that the relation with the actual person is now being mediated through an ever more reinforced image of the other and the freshness goes. As soon as a baby is born people start to talk about them. *'Oh, he looks like his grandfather.'* What does that mean? It means that this new fresh baby is being incorporated into the family narrative. You – an amazing space travelling other – have now been niched inside the family repertoire. *'Ah, we know who you are – just like granddad.'* But a baby is really very strange. Amazing! What to do with a baby? We tell the baby what it is, we domesticate it, we take it into our world. This is what we do all the time.

What I am trying to show with these examples is the difference between consciousness, or the ego's grasping at information to build up pictures about something, and the possibility of having a fresh encounter that allows something new to arise and for us to perhaps find something new in ourselves.

This is why mastery is a delusion. The real masters are always learning and true mastery is a kind of innocence, a freshness of possibility. The master conductor of the orchestra can always find something new to bring out from the piece of music. This is the quality of the primordial buddha – always fresh – not heaped on top of a mountain of accumulated knowledge, but uncovered, revealed.

Verse 1 says, **'the unitary path of primordial purity of awareness and emptiness spreads.'** This means that this awareness is inseparable from emptiness. Emptiness here means ungraspability. You can grasp your ear or your nose but you can't grasp the air in front of you. You make the same gesture but you won't have anything in your hand; there is nothing to get. Of course we are breathing in and out so air is here and without that we die. So 'emptiness' does not mean nothing at all, rather it is emptiness in terms of any fixed definable entity.

There is experience and the space for experience to reveal itself...and then the next moment... and the next moment. This is what is meant by spreading, a continuing unfolding. Nuden Dorje says this emptiness spreads as the spontaneous wisdom free of all relative positions. These relative positions are the structure of binary oppositions: good, bad, right, wrong, male, female and so on. We decide that something is this because it is not that. Most definitions operate on the law of exclusion – the excluded 'other' which allows the seeming simplicity of this particular formation. Today is Friday. It is Friday because it's not Thursday or Saturday. What is the Friday-ness of Friday? There is no internal definition of Friday-ness. If you are a catholic it might mean you would eat fish on Friday. What else do you do on Friday? Describing Friday in terms of Friday-ness is very difficult; it is much easier to say, *'It is not Thursday.'*

This is an interpretive function that is operating in our mind a great deal of the time. I am a man because I am not a woman. I am a man because I am not a boy. I am a man because I am not a dog or a fish. *'Well, James, what does it mean to be a man?'* I don't know. There are a lot of books now about masculinity. In London more men are now wearing beards, so maybe if I grew a beard I would be more of a man. What is the essence of manliness? We don't know. But I am not a dog or a cat. This is very important because by focussing on the clarity that comes with excluding the 'not me,' I can hide from myself the confusion of not knowing what the 'me' is. We do that a lot. *'Keep these people out!'*

In Spain you have separatist movements in various parts of the country. People say, *'I'm not Spanish. I am from the Basque country, or from Catalonia or wherever. I only had to learn Spanish in school because of the government in Madrid. Once we get away from them we will speak our own language and this is who we'll be. Nevertheless, the people in your village speak the wrong dialect so they are a bit dangerous. Even in my own village the older people speak in a funny way, so I'm only going to speak to the people who go to my own local café!'*

There is always separation and division. This is how we operate. Pushing away the bad gives a sense of oneself. Aversion and exclusion affirms my sense of self without me having to define who I am. This is the function of these relative positions. Whenever I say, *'I am this and not that,'* it is as if something definite has been achieved, but it's only held in place by the dynamic of exclusion. What Nuden Dorje is saying is that awareness is not like this; awareness is spontaneously and intuitively full of all possibilities and is free of division. These relative positions of self, other, right or wrong are conceptual elaborations which offer the promise of bringing clarity but just increase our confusion.

We are more slippery than an eel; just see how your mind is slithering, turning and moving. Now we have to do something different because we have been trying to catch this mind for a long time, but it cannot be caught. Everything else can be caught, so why not my mind? But your mind isn't like everything else. What is required is a kind of ontological shift from relying on yourself as a seemingly permanent rational subject who looks at the world, to seeing the simultaneous presence of these two aspects of your existence. You are **both** the empty stage upon which the drama of existence occurs, **and** you are the unfolding drama.

As you walk, talk, think, remember or feel happy or sad, all of these are experiences. The quality of experience is that it is fleeting. The fact that it is not solid doesn't mean that it doesn't occur at all; it occurs but not as some-thing. The problem is our fantasy of some-thing-ness. The founding moment of some-thing-ness is 'here I am'. I am someone. But what are we made of? Ever flowing constituents that are ungraspable, ceaselessly patterning and re-patterning.

This is not philosophy or theory. This is an attempt to get close to the actuality of the arising and passing of our lived experience. What we grasp is not life; we grasp *ideas about life*. Who grasps the idea? Other ideas... chasing ideas... and then we die. Where did the ideas come from? If we think about it we can invent any solution. Our ideas come to us from the planet Mars, or our ideas are being pushed into our minds by the Chinese who have developed a thought-machine, our ideas are entirely the fault of our mother... You can invent any idea you like because it is all just ideas about ideas.

The function of meditation is to directly find the ground of the idea – not as something elsewhere, but as the very ground of our own being. We call it the mind, but the word mind has so many associations and interpretations that it is a little bit problematic. We are referring to mind here as the basic noetic capacity, which means the capacity to display experience. It is not about thinking because thoughts are experiences illuminated by the mind.

Thoughts are like a dictator who has seized power. *"Dear father of the nation, who would we be without you? With humility and gratitude we rejoice on your glorious birthday."* You can spend a lot of time in this wilderness whatever leader you are following. Mao Tse Tung didn't personally free the people of China. Stalin didn't personally transform Russian society, but everything is taken from the ordinary people and projected into the great leader. In the same way, everything is projected into our thoughts and we start to believe that our thoughts are the basis of our identity.

When my mother was getting old and forgetful, sometimes when she visited a doctor he might ask, *'What day of the week is this?'* In the British medical system, if you don't know that Friday is Friday, it's not looking good for you. She was smiling and looking out of her eyes and it didn't matter to her what day of the week it was. The doctor worked Monday to Friday so Friday was important to him but my mother did not work. On a Sunday she would go to church. I would look at my mother's face, and then I would look at the face of the doctor, and I thought my mother was doing better than the doctor! She was certainly much happier. But if you can't think about these things, then who are you? This is the over-privileging of conceptual elaboration. When my mother would see a blackbird in the garden she would be very happy. She was touched and moved by seeing her grandchildren. This is life; we are here and something is happening.

The commentarial domain or aspect of our mental life is important but it's not the king or the queen. It is a usurper of the throne and it's best to send it back to the salt mines!

Verse 2: General Instructions

Letting go of the unnecessary

'Relying on the Guru who shows you the definite meaning, having correctly received the initiations, permissions and instructions, in an isolated place you should initially purify your mind during four or six daily sessions according to the requirements of your own condition.'

'Relying on the Guru who shows you the definite meaning, having correctly received the initiations, permissions and instructions,' This means being willing to reach out from the closed world of your own thoughts to a new possibility. Receiving the transmission means opening yourself to hearing something new. It is not that you magically get something given by someone else, but rather that you start to put yourself into question. It is not about finding out about how to go from here to there, but starting to see that being here — where we always are — is hidden from us by our thoughts about being here.

We start to become a little suspicious of our assumptions. An idea or a thought comes into our mind. Is it really true? Or is it just a thought? By this sensitivity to the possibility that thoughts are misleading the thought is moved from the place of truth and necessity to the place of potential.

In the pizzeria the chef has many little pots with different kinds of delicious ingredients. The order comes in for a particular pizza and the chef takes from the appropriate pot the ingredients required for that kind of pizza. Because of the specific request for the pizza the potential present in all the ingredients is still there, but only the potential of certain ingredients is activated; the other ingredients sit quietly in their pots. They are good ingredients but, *'No thank you, I don't want mushrooms on my pizza marinara as it's not appropriate, so please don't put them on.'* They are perfectly good mushrooms but we don't need them for this pizza. Life sends an order to us: please participate in this way. *'But I don't want to participate in this way because I like participating in that way.'* That way is lovely too but it's not what was asked for.

When you see this in yourself – you serve other people something they don't want, you say things that upset them that they didn't even need to hear – this is not being connected with the world. You were acting from an assumption: because it feels right for me you should have it even if you don't want it. If I give you something you don't want you are not going to say thank you. I don't want to hear you saying, *'No thank you,'* since if you loved me you would appreciate me telling you this even if you don't want to hear it. *'No, I am not saying I know what is good for you, but I just think you should hear what I need to say.'* We know these stories because we are caught up in something – an obsession – a need to do it like this.

What Nuden Dorje is referring to here is the teaching which allows you to do less. It is not about building up a huge knowledge of buddhist dharma; it is about responding to the situation as is required by the situation, so that what arises in you is fitting because the focus of your attention is on what is here and now. Not on what might be or what I want it to be, but on this actual situation. We usually understand learning as a process of accumulating and building up information, but in this approach the path is about letting go of the unnecessary.

Then he continues in Verse 2: **'In an isolated place you should initially purify your mind during four or six daily sessions according to the requirements of your own condition.'**

How do we do this purification? What is it that has to be purified?

First of all, we have to know what is making our mind dirty. When the cars drive by on the road they are making the road dirty as they fill the space of the road, but before you can stop them they have driven away. Even a very dirty car driving by has gone, and a bright shiny clean car has also gone. *'I don't want dirty cars driving on this road. I spend a lot of money coming to this lovely place in the country, and I don't want to look out of the window and see dirty cars. I am going to block the road and preach to the drivers of these cars the virtues of cleaning their cars. Unfortunately, this will bring me into closer contact with dirty cars, but it's worth it.'* This is what happens when you try to control your own mind. *'I don't want these kinds of thoughts in my mind. I am not going to tolerate it. I am going to stop them.'* Difficult. Actually, the thoughts come and go.

The slow path is to try to purify your thoughts. The problem is how do you catch a thought? You can wash your socks. You take them off your feet and put them in the basin with some soap and rub them about. You have socks, water, hands and soap, so you can do it. Okay, so now we are going to wash our thoughts. How do we catch a thought? They are gone very quickly. You have to be quicker than the thought, and they are slippery wrigglers.

Regardless of whether you say this is a good thought or a bad thought it has gone, and this is what it means in the text by 'purifying your thoughts'. To see the natural intrinsic purity of everything which arises and passes in the mind is the purification of the thought. This is the vital central principle in dzogchen. It is not that this dirty bad thought is contaminating you, it is that you have a thought about a thought: *'I don't want to have thoughts like this in my mind.'* This thought about a thought acts as a glue that binds you onto the bad thought and so you are endlessly getting tangled trying to make your mind the way you want it to be. The thought as an actuality is always vanishing. The essence of the practice is to stay present with whatever is arising, and if we do that we see that each arising is effortlessly vanishing.

Since you woke up this morning you have had hundreds of thousands of thoughts and sensations. They have appeared and vanished and whether you liked them or not, they have gone. As we looked earlier, a child saying that some food is horrible and refusing to eat it is a double move, which the child has to realise is not valid. *'I don't like this and therefore I am going to say it's horrible.'* It is not horrible because other people do eat it – it's just that you just don't like it. In the same way with your mind you have some thoughts or sensations that you don't like. Are they horrible? You don't like them. Does that make them horrible? Whether you like them or not they arise and pass. *'But they're horrible and I don't want to have any more thoughts like that.'* You, with your own mind, are putting yourself in prison. The thought has gone. It's like saying that's a horrible rainbow or a horrible echo because you can't catch it. When you say it's horrible you are the one creating the seemingly enduring essential substantial truth of this object.

Having made it dirty you now have to clean it, but maybe it wasn't dirty in the first place; maybe it was a sad thought or a mean thought or a cruel thought or a selfish thought and that is what is was. I have a cruel thought – I want you to suffer – but I'm a buddhist so I shouldn't have a thought like that. Now I am having non-buddhist thoughts and this is very bad. 'I want you to suffer' is a thought. Only if I identify with my energy into the thought does the thought become real for me. Thoughts arise in the mind but to think that it's *my* mind and I should or could control what happens in my mind is a big mistake.

The mind is like a public park where there are dogs running around, children kicking footballs, people drinking beer under the trees; all kinds of things are happening. If you go up to the people playing football and say, *'Listen, I don't like people playing football here. I am having a nice time in the park so please stop playing football.'* I don't think they will agree. It is the same in your own mind. Thoughts arise, it's a public park, and they come and they go. Who is causing trouble? You are causing trouble for yourself by saying, *'It is not a public park, it is my mind. I am going to put a wall around it. I am going to plant flowers and hang a hammock between the trees and just relax and enjoy myself. But hey, now the neighbour's cat is coming in and shitting in the corner. This is outrageous! I am going to telephone the thought police to come and sort this out.'*

In buddhism, we have Dorje Sempa, and he is the big washerman. If you phone him he will come and clean anything dirty but he can't stop the dirt from coming. The more you become attentive to the dirt, the more you develop allergies: can't eat this; can't wear that; can't go there; very difficult. What Nuden Dorje is saying here in a very condensed form is *'Recognise the nature of the mind.'* The mind is not a private possession. You can control what your hand does but you can't control your thoughts. What you can control is whether you enact the thought.

Tomorrow we will start by doing some dzogchen meditation practice, which is a way of allowing ourselves the freedom to be with ourselves however we are. All the Buddha's teachings are about the middle way – not too tight, not too loose. Don't worry, if you open your mind you are not going to be invaded or overwhelmed by anything. There is enough space for everything. All we have to do is to keep relaxing our habitual compulsion to try to establish control. In different cultures at different times people have developed many methods for trying to control their mind and a lot of these methods involve putting pressure on oneself, which is likely to encourage guilt and shame. The way of dzogchen is different. Dzogchen says that from the very beginning the mind is completely pure; all seeming impurities are adventitious arising due to causes and circumstances. If you sit calmly and observe these obscurations or limitations or negative thoughts they don't stay; they are just passing through.

In 1968, I went hitchhiking down through Morocco through Spanish Sahara and into Mauritania. For Spanish Sahara I got a safe passage permit which meant I could come in, but I must go out. There was no permission to remain – just passing through. This is what you need in the immigration office of your mind. When the thought arises – stamp the passport – safe conduct! This is what we will explore tomorrow.

Day Two

Good morning on this beautiful day. Let's begin with some quiet sitting just to settle into the space. We bring our attention to focus on the in and out movement of the breath at the end of the nostrils and that is all we have to do. If we find that our mind gets distracted and we go off wandering after thoughts and feelings then we just very gently bring our attention back to the breath.

The world is already full of people who regard other people as enemies, so don't turn yourself into an enemy and fight with yourself and blame yourself if you don't practise as 'well' as you think you should. The focus of our work is tenderness and gentleness and this carries great clarity, because when we are tender towards ourselves we start to understand ourselves. Just like a parent with a small child, if they do something we don't like there is no point in shouting at them. We have to see what might have caused them to do that and then speak into that pattern. In the same way, judging ourselves as bad, or lazy, or stupid doesn't help, rather we want to see the patterns of how we get lost. Seeing clearly without evaluative judgement is the path.

We will sit for a while.

Shamatha practice

When we do this kind of practice, sometimes we experience our mind as calm, but often there is a lot of movement and turbulence. Like a sailor who has been washed overboard and is being tossed around in the waves we have to find a piece of driftwood to hold on to. If the sailor lets go of the wood he will sink underneath the waves, and in the same way we hold onto the breath as a protection from being pulled this way and that by feelings, thoughts and sensations.

You might even feel that before you came into this room you were quite happy, as you had been walking outside in the sunshine with nice people all around you. You might think that this is a very easy and nice way to spend your time. But when you sit down to meditate your mind seems very confused and difficult. *'Maybe meditation is making me worse, and I should follow the path of coffee in the sunshine.'* Why? What happens when we meditate? We come to encounter the actuality of our subconscious life: our mind is movement which has no fixed direction.

Due to external and internal stimuli we find certain kinds of experience arising, and trying to organise our thoughts and bring them into a smooth direction is very difficult; it's like herding cats. Thoughts don't follow an easy straightforward path. Through this kind of practice we can learn many things, and especially about our urge to impose control. As long as I am in control and can impose order on my life I feel okay, but when the control breaks down I feel anxious and fearful. *'What will happen to me? I will be overwhelmed. I won't know what to do.'*

From the point of view of dzogchen, this primordial fear and anxiety arises due to the illusion of separation. That is to say, 'I, me, myself,' and who I take myself to be feels like an individual. I am me – not you. The term individual means indivisible: it cannot be chopped up, and this gives us the sense that I should be complete as myself. I should know who I am because if I am an individual it shouldn't take too long to find out who I am. But of course we are not an individual; we are a multiplicity that we are not in charge of. Ego or self finds itself after the fact of being, and being reveals itself in ways beyond calculation. The ego retreats into the search for domination and control; a totalising function which then leads to a totalitarian discourse: a dictatorship.

We can see everywhere in the world a very strong relationship between fear and anxiety and military rule. It is as if we will only be safe if we can control our enemies. Many forms of meditation such as tantric visualisations and purification practices exist inside that paradigm. *'I am going to do this. I can learn this special technique that will make this happen.'* The driving force is fear and danger.

The view in dzogchen is different because it says that from the very beginning our own nature is complete; not complete as a totalising knowable function, but as an infinite awareness. And so the path is to take refuge in ourselves as we are, because our true nature is not different from the Buddha.

For example, if you are out in the country having a nice walk and you see dark clouds blowing towards you and suddenly heavy rain starts to fall, you want to find some refuge. You love flowers, but if you go to a little daisy it won't give you much protection. You see a big oak tree and so you run to the tree and now you feel dry. The oak tree offers protection just by being an oak tree and all you have to do is be where the protection is. You are not making the protection; you put yourself in the way of the protection.

THE MIND IS THE MATRIX

In dzogchen it says, *'I take refuge in my own mind.'* When we are at school learning about languages and poetry we learn about the cadences of languages and how we can change the meaning of a sentence by where we put the stress. *'I'* take refuge in my mind. *I* am so big and I have my mind. There is a problem here because *I* am bigger than my mind. *I* put my mind on top of my head but the rain is still coming down! So what is meant is more like, ' I take refuge in my mind; the mind is very big and there is a place for everything; thoughts, feelings, memories, hopes, fears and so on. '

Since we were born we have existed as a flow of experience and this experience has occurred for us because we have a mind. The mind is the clarity that shows the ever-changing movement of experience. Experience seems to be impactful – it seems to register – and because of that it has a felt sense of importance; something is there. You feel tired, or hungry, or wanting to see what's in the market, and this is all quite energising and formative. It gives us something to relate to. *'Oh, later on, during the break, I'll go to the market.'* There is something to think about. But the mind – where is it? The mind is the facilitative matrix and without the mind we wouldn't have the experience; it is the ground, or the basis, or the mother, but what we attend to is the flow of experience.

Experience arises in two linked modalities: subject and object, or self and other. Our life is dialogic and is a continuous conversation between these voices which sometimes appear to be subject and sometimes appear to be object. If we think about some problem at work as being hopeless, it is as if the subject dissolves into the object situation. If we say, *'I am really angry about this, and I am not going to put up with this!'* It is as if the situation is pulled into the subject and the subject is going to be making some changes, and so our experience of the world is moving between these two polarities. Both are movements. Whatever you take to be your subjective self is a composition, a coming together of many different factors creating pattern after pattern.

In the space of the self many different patterns or contents exist. Our self is not a thing but a space of potential located inside the space of awareness, therefore, when we say 'I take refuge in my mind', we are saying that this space of me being me, which seems to be like a bubble of private existence, is inside the big space. For example, with small children you can take a piece of wire and some washing up liquid and you can blow bubbles. What is a bubble? Air outside and air inside with a very thin skin; the inside and the outside are not different. But we look, and we say, *'Oh, look at the bubbles!'* as if something was there. This is our self. We are just a bubble. What is outside and what is inside is the same. The world is made of chemicals, and we are also made of chemicals.

ADAPTING TO THE WORLD

From the buddhist point of view, our sufferings, difficulties, and confusions all arise from ignorance and this is not a fixed state but an active movement of ignoring. What are we ignoring? How it is. In order to ignore 'how it is' we fantasise how we think it is. Each of us creates our own notion of the world; our purpose, what our life is for, what's important and what's not important. This is our activity. We are constructing a world according to our own effort and interest, and we live in a time where due to the orientation of consumerist capitalism we have many, many possibilities.

There are many people in this room but nobody is wearing exactly the same clothes. When Mao Tse Tung was in charge in China, five hundred million people were all wearing identical blue suits, but here we are not wearing the same things because we are exerting our right to choose. *'This is what I like. I express myself with my shirt, and my shirt is the basis for my identity.'* It helps that there are so many choices of clothes. We are constructing our identity and there is no end to it as there is always something more to buy.

Due to the blessed power of gravity the ageing skin starts to wrinkle. Luckily for us, many creams are available, but some of these creams are very expensive. You can pay one hundred and fifty euros for a tiny pot of Crème de la Mer, and then you need to have a magnifying glass to see if it has made any difference! This is because there is always something to be done. Our world is doing...doing...doing...

In the Tibetan language the normal word for a sentient being is *drowa*. It is both a noun and a verb and it means to go, but also a goer – a moving event. Since we were born we have been moving and turning and changing, trying to get rid of things we don't like and trying to get things we do like.

In the dzogchen tradition, in the lineage coming down from the primordial buddha, Kuntuzangpo, our mind is without beginning and end; it has no colour or shape and it is not covered by anything; t is naked, raw and fresh, not cooked by anything. When we think of our personality or our individual self it is very cooked. You are cooked in your family, in school, at college, at work, and also with friends and lovers. There is a lot of encouragement to be in particular ways so we modify and change ourselves trying to find a niche where we can fit, but of course there is a great deal of artificiality in this.

If we have made ourselves in a particular way due to the operation of our intention – our mobilised energy and the environmental factors around us – what we have is a construct. However the Buddha said, all compounded things are impermanent: you put factors together and they work for a while, and then they don't work and it starts to fall apart.

I was watching some of the market stallholders setting up their stalls this morning and it's a lot of work. Maybe two hours to set everything out, then selling for three or four hours and then they pack everything back in the van. It is a transient festival, but that is the same for all of us. You get up in the morning, you get out of bed, you have a shower and put on your clothes and you go to work. You come home from work, you take your clothes off and you go to bed. Each day we are establishing the little market of ourselves and we hope somebody will be interested in what we are offering. Sometimes, at the end of the day, you have to pack it all up even though you didn't sell anything. This is life and it has to be like this. Why? Because it is the nature of activity.

Dzogchen points to two aspects of the mind. There is the mind of space – open, present awareness – the natural clarity or capacity to show. This is the mind itself. But the mind also shows many different forms. This is the play of its energy. These forms are always changing. We have the stillness of spacious openness, *kyewa mepa* in Tibetan, meaning unborn. It means that the space of the mind is not a thing that you can grasp or hold on to and yet it is the ground or basis or source of all these energetic forms that are arising. The flow of experience never stops and cannot be stopped because it flows like a river. What is still is not the flow and what is flowing is not the stillness, but the stillness and the flow are inseparable.

When we lose the presence of the spacious ground of our being we find that all we are conscious of is the movement and we end up in this hopeless task of trying to stabilise the movement. But movement is movement – it is not stable – so this is destined to disappoint. *'I want to sort my life out. I really need to think about what I am going to do in the next five years. I am going to come up with a plan for the future, and then I am going to make sure it happens the way I want it to.'* This is a very popular madness because it seldom happens the way we plan, which is not to say that we shouldn't plan. It fails not because we are lazy, stupid or bad, but because of a fundamental ontological confusion: the moving doesn't stop moving.

If you want stillness you have to look where the stillness is; the stillness is not far away but it doesn't look like movement. Movement is moving. We are used to looking at movement. The kind of orientation in yourself that is required to see movement will not reveal stillness. We experience movement by participating in movement. We do things; we tidy the house, or we cook something in the kitchen. We know how to take something from the fridge and to prepare some food. This is the choreography of our existence; the ballet of everyday life. It is very beautiful to observe movement like watching the people putting up their market stalls. One minute somebody is stretching up to pull up an awning, and then they are bending down to lift up a box and put it on the table. The subject and the object move together to create patterns of shape and each of us does this all day long.

To put on my trousers I have to stand on one leg. When I was four years of age that was quite difficult. When I was forty that was very easy, but now I am sixty-seven that is more difficult so the choreography is not quite so elegant!

This is our life – movement and change. There is nothing wrong with movement, but if you seek stability, security and profound clarity, you won't find it in the ceaseless unfolding of existence. We have to find a way to enter the stillness which is always already there; it is not about making something or doing something or creating something. Our mind has been here from the very beginning. You cannot lose or find it because it is not a possession – a thing you have or don't have – t is the very basis of your existence of being alive and of having experience.

In the traditional example it is like the mirror. When you look in a mirror you see a reflection you don't see the mirror. The mirror shows itself through the reflection. The mirror is an empty spacious clarity which reveals its quality through the display of reflection. And so if we want to know that there is a mirror we don't look for the mirror as something like a reflection, but we see that the reflection shows the presence of the mirror by the absence of the mirror as something. The mirror is showing itself through its absence of being something.

For example, here we have a book with a picture on the cover. This picture shows itself again and again. In a sense, it demonstrates its something-ness – it is this – and if I turn it around it is pretty much the same thing as it gets more or less light on it depending on whether it faces the window, but it's still the cover of the book. But a mirror has no something-ness of its own. The mirror shows the other as self. The reflection is not the mirror. The mirror is like the mind. Our mind is not a thing, it is a potential of showing, and if that potential were already filled with itself it would only show itself, just like the cover of the book shows the cover of the book. But our mind shows many possibilities and on a relative level we are aware of this.

In terms of the first person singular I can say that I am tired, I am hungry, I am happy, I am sad. It is possible to say each of these things because none of them is eternally true; they are situationally true. Due to causes and conditions I feel tired or happy or hungry. In the moment that is occurring I say, *'I'm tired.'* One hundred percent true. *'Really, you must believe me, I'm tired.'* And then I have a rest and I don't feel tired. *'Let's go for a walk.'* "But I thought you were tired." *'I was tired, but now ...'* This is ourself showing so many things because we are not one definite thing, and this gives us the flavour of the mind.

The mind shows many different possibilities because it is nothing, but it is not nothing at all; it is the facilitative nothing – the plenum void – the void or the space which effortlessly and instantly is showing. What I take myself to be at any moment is a patterning of energy, or experience, or shaping, which is valid as experience but it is not an eternal truth. This is the mysterious nature of our existence. Whenever we say something true about ourself we are also saying something false because these formations which we are, are situational. We are called into being by the constellation of the factors of the environment.

In March, last year, I retired from working in the public health system. I had that job because of the kind of training and knowledge I have, and up until now I haven't forgotten too many of the things I knew then. But if I now go into the clinic, they ask, *'Oh, James, what are you doing here?'* I worked there for twenty-five years and I know that place very well, but now if I go in they ask me why I'm here? My old colleagues are friendly but a bit surprised. I can't just go into the waiting room and decide to talk to a patient!

The context has changed as it is no longer a stage on which I can manifest whatever knowledge and qualities I have in the realm of therapy, and so the experience that I have built up over the years becomes latent. While I was going to work it appeared to be me but that was because of the situation. I was only being me in the clinic because of having a job contract. This is our life. Different situations call us into being in particular ways. The richness of our lives depends on the richness of our context. The more situations we can be open to, the more aspects of our lives are allowed to come forward and to start to flourish.

This is another way of saying that there is no me; there is me plus situations and the situation invites me or doesn't invite me to manifest particular aspects. That is to say, our energy and the world's energy are moving together because it is actually a single field of experience. To put this in another way, in mahayana buddhism, we talk of two aspects, wisdom and compassion. Wisdom is to understand emptiness: the fact that there is no essence or defining substance in any phenomena and that everything arises due to causes and conditions.

Last night, Juan and I walked up to the little castle. We were looking down on this very beautiful town. We could see a row of half-built houses – the foundations looked fine but due to the economic crisis the building work had stopped. We see these poor walls breaking. They are naked into the wind and rain because they are not finished, but then we walk around and we see other houses and they seem to be something because they look so nice. The walls are painted white but if they weren't painted they wouldn't be white; they are not white forever. Everything is moving. If you have to clean your home you know that dust arrives by itself – it's always there. In the same way change is occurring in everything we see, and this is life.

Our life is movement in the field of movement. The way to live well is to learn to move well, to be flexible, and to accept that change is normal. When we try to hold on to situations then we feel the friction and the grinding. We start to feel it shouldn't be like this because I have an idea of how it should be, but we are not living in a world of ideas, we live in the actual world. The plan that these builders had of building a row of houses is interrupted by the bank; it's a nice idea but if you have no money you won't be able to sell these houses.

Our life is interruption, change, and frustration, which is increased by our non-acceptance that life is difficult. What now? If we are open, what shall we do? We can't go this way, so what shall we do? We will go that way. *'Oh, but I wanted to go this way. I am sure I should go this way. Life would be better if I went this way.'* But you can't go that way, you can go this way. *'But I don't want to go that way. I want to go this way.'* This is the royal road to suffering in which your own intelligence in developing plans and patterns finds itself in opposition to the emergent shape of circumstances. The exit from this kind of conflict is to stay with the integration of the flow of experience and the basic space within which it's moving. By resting in space there is contentment because space doesn't need anything else, and the flow of experience is a gesture out of connectivity within the shared field of becoming. In that way, we can trust our intuition and we can be more spontaneous.

Of course, if you are planning a holiday, or you are going to do a big shop for the week ahead, you need to know what you need to buy. If you are going to cook, the main thing to consider is the ingredients. The recipe is the servant of the ingredients. If you start with a recipe that requires red onions and they only have white onions in the market, you are not so happy when you cook as it's not going to be so good. Throw away the recipe. Smell the white onions. What are the ingredients? What is the topology? What is the direct phenomenology of our existence? How to cook with what we have because what we have is what we get. All sorts of things happen in our lives: sickness, unemployment, loneliness, confusion, difficulty in relationships, sick parents, wayward children. We have to manage to find a way. This is not to say that experience is unimportant, but if it is made over important by being the real truth of my life then like a cork on the water we are going up and down with these waves of events.

Therefore, recognising the always already integration of space and movement is the heart of dzogchen. The mind is primordially pure because there is nothing to be marked. If we had the cover of a book we could write on it with a big pen, and then we might think it is spoiled as something bad has happened to it. But if you think of the mirror, no matter what kind of reflection arises in the mirror it doesn't spoil the mirror. Something horrible is being reflected in the mirror but it doesn't change the mirror, and that is what is meant by primordial purity; not that it is something held apart or away from life. The thing about the mirror is that it has a very intimate relation with the reflection. The reflection is inside the mirror and yet it doesn't touch the mirror.

All of our experiences are in our mind – immediate and direct – but it doesn't leave a mark. What is marked is the pattern of energy I call, 'I, me, myself.' The ego or the self is a patterning of energy and it gets bumped by the events of existence and so we have hopes and fears. We feel expansive or contractive. We are marked by life as a person, but we are not just this person. The ground of our personhood is our awareness, so we are both the mirror *and* the reflection – the space *and* the manifestation – and awakening to the always-present integration of these two is enlightenment, as considered in the dzogchen tradition.

MEDITATION: THE ACTIVITY OF NON-ACTIVITY

The basic focus of the meditation practice is to relax into the openness of the mind. You might think that this would be very easy to do but actually we spend most of our time being busy: I, the subject, am going to do something to the object. We exist as a kind of organisation of energy. For example, if you are going to clean your teeth you have to unscrew the toothpaste, squeeze it onto the brush – not too little – not too much – put the top back on the toothpaste, and get the brush into your mouth. All of this involves intention and the intention becomes the organising factor to mobilise energy in the necessary patterning.

Buddhism has many activities that involve intention but this practice is not that kind of activity; it is the activity of non-activity. You simply relax and allow experience to arise and pass. You can enter into this experience in different ways. The simplest way is just to relax into the out breath. We do it by sitting in a relaxed way with the skeleton carrying our weight so the muscles can be relaxed. Generally, we do it with the hands on the knees, which is a very open way of sitting. The chin is slightly raised and our gaze is open and resting into the space in front of us. One of the aspects that we want to relax is our maintenance of the sense of separation between self and other. Everything is our experience. Experience doesn't mean that it is a fantasy of the mind; it means that what is occurring arising as smells, sounds, tastes, thoughts, feelings and sensations, each has its own particular formation and impact and we just sit and allow the movement of the mind.

As we looked before the break, the mind is space and movement. The ego self is part of the movement; a part which sets itself apart from the other aspects so we sit inside this bubble of self-reference. We want to relax out of that limitation because the ego formation is already inside the mirror of the mind. When we are sitting, occurrences and appearances are happening and sometimes it looks outside and sometimes it looks inside; just allow it to occur. The key thing that we are relaxing away from is our habit of making sense of the world.

You might hear some sound outside and you wonder what is happening. You don't need to know. You just have a sound. *'But what does that sound mean?'* The most important thing it means is that you are not dead so be happy to be alive. There is sound and colour – it's enough. *'But why? How? What are they doing?'* This takes you back into this little bubble of yourself. *'I need to know because if I don't know who knows what could happen?'* In that moment you can experience the retroactive anxiety that is causing you to cut off from the world. Relax – it is just stuff – it is there and then it's gone. You don't need to interfere with it. In fact the less you interfere with it, the less it will interfere with you. In that way the compulsion to organise starts to relax.

Sitting practice

We will do this practice for quite a short period of time. The reason we do it for short periods is because we have a lot of deep-rooted subtle tendencies to act. We may start relaxed but usually we become a little busier because the ego is saying, *'Hey, what about me?'* We are offering early retirement to the ego, but the ego doesn't know how to be retired. The ego needs to be busy, to have its own identity, and this is why we will probably notice ourselves fusing into thought forms. The basic meditation instruction is not to push away thoughts or feelings or sensations that you don't like, and not to try and hang on to thoughts and feelings that you do like. The ego is improved by good thoughts but the mind isn't! Think back to the image of the mirror; if something beautiful is reflected in the mirror, the mirror itself is not improved. Whether the mirror is reflecting something ugly or beautiful it is still just a reflection, although if we see a beautiful reflection we probably do want to look some more.

This is the heart of the practice. When we say, *'I don't want this thought in my mind because I am big and the mind is my possession'*, we see that the mind is very big and more generous than me. My mind is willing to welcome things that my ego doesn't want to welcome. Again and again we relax into the spaciousness of the mind, and then gradually these habit formations of organising and controlling start to subside and have less meaning. And then we have freedom, because now we can be present with the unfolding world and respond to what is here, and not to what was or what we would like to be.

Okay, so sitting in a comfortable way relaxing into the out breath we stay open and present to whatever is occurring.

Some of you may be familiar with vipassana meditation, particularly the practice of scanning through the body and seeing the basic arising moments before they are captured within conceptual elaboration. You can think of the practice we have just been doing as a kind of vipassana, because as we are sitting the room is arising, our body is arising, and memories are arising. If we are present with what is arising it is here but ungraspable. However when we take it to be something like 'this is my back' or 'I am here inside my body', then this thought creates a kind of consolidation on the basis of which we build up a little palace of thoughts.

By returning again and again to the present moment of the arising and passing, you can see directly that this body is not a thing but is a flow of experience. The room is not a thing but is a flow of experience, and it is the same with cars, the market, the hills, the town and the people; you can grasp them as thoughts or you can be with them in their immediacy as transient events.

This is the basic division between what is called samsara and nirvana. When you grasp at something what you get is not a thing because there is no thing, you get a concept. When you don't grasp everything is still here; the world is not annihilated. The world is just doing itself. The ego is not so important; it is not the centre of the world. The mind is the centre of the world. It is a very simple and profound practice and the more you do it, the more you see the richness in it.

Now we will go back to the text.

Verse 3: Meditation about Samsara

'In this world appearance is ceaselessly flowing; in this ocean of poison there is no time to seek liberation. We wander again and again in the six realms of samsara and no matter what we try we always experience suffering with no chance of happiness.'

He is pointing here to how the world appears when we are operating inside the paradigm of duality and attachment. Events are occurring. What do they mean? What are they for? Yesterday we began talking about the five skandhas, the five organising factors. Something arises which has a negative feeling tone for us and on that basis we conclude it's bad. Feeling that something is bad, we try to get rid of it. If something feels pleasant we conclude it's good and because it is good we try to get more of it. This basic pulsation of seeking what we like and getting rid of what we don't like is the way the ego formation feels increased or decreased by the quality of the objects it has access to.

He says we are swimming in this ocean of poisons. Poison here means the five basic afflictions. The first is a kind of stupidity or mental dullness: the assumption that I exist as something concrete with my own essence and substance as does everything else. On the basis of this we have attraction, desire, aversion, anger, pride, jealousy and envy, and many other ways of positioning. When we like something we think it's special and when we don't like something we think it is dreadful and this feels real, true, and important. But other people like things we don't like and other people don't like things we do like, therefore, the feeling tone that arises of something being horrible is not a truth about the object but is the quality of our mental formation in that moment. This is our mind at work, however we think it is the object. That is why Nuden Dorje describes us as swimming in an ocean of poison. Trying to avoid things that are difficult, and trying to get more of what we like, we are tossed around in these waves of whatever is occurring at the moment.

Being busy trying to manage our lives gives us no time for liberation because there is always something to be done. When I retired from the hospital, I had all sorts of plans about what I would be doing with my free time, but I don't find much free time since there is always something to be busy with! At the end of the day I am tired, thinking what did I do? The days and months and years go by: old age, sickness and death.

So, if we are waiting for some free time in which to do our sacred holy practice we are going to be waiting for a long time! That is why we need to integrate the practice into the arising of whatever is occurring. Daily life itself is the practice and that is why we focus on observing our own mind. Experiences like jealousy or pride or loneliness or sadness are not obstacles to practice but they are the very focus of the practice.

By being present as a space of hospitality, like the mirror, we allow this formation to be there. the more we do that the more we develop the relaxed confidence that we will not be contaminated by these so-called poisons. If we are jealous, we are just jealous. If we don't build it up into a big story it is just a flavour and then it goes. Now we can be at home in the world as it is.

Some of you might know the vajra, the symbol of emptiness. It has little side points coming out, emerging from the mouth of a sea creature called a *makara*, a huge sea monster which can swallow everything. This is a symbol for emptiness. Emptiness can swallow everything. Everything goes into emptiness, but not much goes into the ego. This is the freedom that comes from finding the open, empty, spacious mind. You can be with your life as it is.

Last week, I had to go to the hospital to have a scan. I had to go into a little room and change out of my clothes into a little hospital robe. The robes are standard size, but I am a little bit bigger than standard size. I put on my little robe and then I had to go out into the waiting room. Sitting opposite me was a woman and her daughter. When I sat down it seemed my little robe was opening up so I had to sit in an awkward position and it took quite a lot of effort to sit like this, especially because I had been told to drink a litre of water just before the scan! I said to the nurse, *'Look, listen, I am getting old and my bladder is full and I am not very comfortable so can we go through quite quickly?'* She said, 'Well, today there is quite a queue.' This is my life as a human being – just this. You get sick and you go into the hospital... When you are outside walking down the street you are a citizen, but when you go through the door of the hospital you are a patient. You have become very small. You sit and you wait and you have to be grateful for what you get. This is our existence, so we have to find a way to accept that this is it, because it is always just this, however it is. We could perhaps make it more efficient by doing one thing or another, however it will always be just this. The function of the practice is not to fight with life and also not to be defeated by life or to become a victim, but whatever is happening – here I am. Right here.

Nuden Dorje goes on to say, **'We wander again and again in the six realms of samsara and no matter what we try we always experience suffering with no chance of happiness.'** Frustration is built into the structure of duality. In being separated from the environment around me – if I approach it from a distance – my experience is mediated by the thoughts I have about it, hence my own intelligence is the basis of my persecution.

While I was sitting waiting in the hospital, I started thinking that I should have a word with the manager of the ward because it is a terrible way to organise this facility. However since I have worked in the health system I know what the manager will say: *'Thank you so much for your helpful idea which I will put in the wastepaper bin.'* My thoughts telling me about the faults of the situation change nothing and only distress myself. This is a waste of mental energy. So much of the time we have anxieties and worries and dissatisfaction which make no improvements to the situation and just create turbulence. These moments are very important where we see we are the cause of our own distress. When we relax we see that this is how it is.

When I first lived in India I had to make regular train journeys from Calcutta to Delhi. The local train took thirty-six hours and it was often twenty-four hours late. This is a very long journey. At first I would think, *'Why have we stopped here? The train has stopped in the middle of nowhere – why? What is going on?'* I tried to ask the Indian people what was happening and they just said, *'Who knows?'* Not only who knows, but who cares?! After some years it became like that for me too; the train stopped, you looked out the window, and you watched a cow. 'We are not moving' was just a fact. India is a great blessing place for this reason.

Nowadays, with efficiency being the great god of capitalism, people are always trying to remove problems, but I don't see any signs that we have fewer problems. Problems are embedded in duality. Rather than being surprised or outraged or trying to change problems, by accepting the problem we have the best possibility of changing things in a useful way. By seeing the problem as an obstacle or a curse or a form of sabotage or the work of demons we just disturb ourselves.

The six realms of samsara cover all the possibilities where one could be born: the god realms, the jealous god realms, the human realms, the animal realms, the hungry ghost realms and hell realms. All of these are the possibilities generated by mental content. We exist in our form because we believe in the content of our mind. If a human being starts barking like a dog people will be upset. Yesterday afternoon I was looking down from my room onto a path where there a mother, a father, and a small child were walking. The child was walking quite steadily but a little crazily. I felt so envious of this small child because he was walking along making crazy sounds, but as an adult I'm not allowed to do that. This little child had absolute freedom to do whatever he wanted, but if we did this we'd wonder that others might think us mad. This is how we get full of particular patterns of behaviour. The anxiety about how we will appear to the mind of another breeds the artificiality of our adult life, and because of this we retain thought formations which give rise to the possibilities of birth in different realms.

Verse 4: The Opportunity of This Life

'Your body is the remnant of the karma you have not yet exhausted. It is the site of the freedoms and blessings which are so difficult to obtain. Having gained this precious human existence, a good base free of faults, so hard to get, so easy to destroy, you must quickly become diligent in the practice of virtue.'

From this buddhist point of view what we have as our lot in body, health, and flexibility, is generated out of causes which we created a long time ago. It is not a matter of mere luck. We have accumulated some good karma or resourcing out of our ethical behaviour in the past because, as we discussed yesterday, 'I' as the first person singular has no content of its own.

If you go out in the fields and you see some cows, when they recognise you they will walk towards you because cows are very social. Maybe you pick some nice fresh grass for them and they look at you with their big eyes and you see all the flies around their eyes. This is a living sentient being full of cow-ness, just as we are full of human-ness. The 'I' is able to identify itself as a cow or a dog or a bird or a human, and due to causes and conditions we find ourselves born in these different realms.

Whether you believe this or not, if you just hold it as a working hypothesis, what it indicates is the dynamic nature of our existence. It is not that I am a human being, but that moment-by-moment I have experiences mediated through the dimension of being human. This is how the world appears for a human body and this is a flow of experience. After a while we will die, and if everything doesn't just stop when we die something will go on taking a new form depending on the nature of its impulses and what it is drawn towards. And then another life begins. This is what the text is indicating here.

The resources which give rise to this opportunity of being in a human body are already being used up. There are many more insects in the world than human beings. It is like buying a lottery ticket; not many people win, most people lose. Statistically, the chance of being reborn as an insect is much greater than the chance of being reborn as a human. *'But how could I be reborn as an insect?! I am me. I am a human being'* But being a human being doesn't protect us very much. In Africa and the Middle East, we read stories of young girls being taken away and sold as slaves. The dignity or the guarantees of the United Nations Declaration of Human Rights doesn't protect them. We are at the mercy of forces all around us. We can say this is our luck or our karma, but the factors that keep us safe and the factors that bring our death, our destruction, or our harm, are always in dynamic dialogue.

"This body is the site of the freedoms and blessings which are so difficult to obtain. Having gained this precious human existence; a good base free of faults, so hard to get and so easy to destroy; you must quickly become diligent in the practice of virtue."

One of the advantages of being in a human body is that we have access to understanding the various possibilities of life. In the tradition it describes how in the god realms life is easy; there is always plenty to eat and it's pleasant. Today is a nice Saturday and people are sitting outside chatting to their friends. The sun is shining and there are no problems... for a while. However there are still people working in the dark, down in coal mines where the tunnels may collapse. Fishermen go out to sea where there are storms and they have to use dangerous equipment in the cold. Many kinds of things can go wrong, but on a good day when the sun is shining we think we will be happy for ever. Nuden Dorje is inviting us to reflect on how everything arises from causes and conditions, how nothing is guaranteed by an internal essence or substance. Our situation is fragile – it is a time to do something – we have a chance to observe our mind.

When you see cats on the street they are usually looking around for food. I have never seen a cat admire a flower. They have a limited area of interest: sex and killing. We have a little bit more scope and we can think, *'Who is the one who wants to have sex?'* When we have the arising of this feeling, what is its nature? I don't think small birds or the cows in the field have this capacity. The cow has four legs but it doesn't know how to open the gate to get out of the field. The cows and the horses are owned by someone. The bird is free but at the mercy of many things that can kill it. When we look around at the many different forms of life we can see how fortunate we are, and we can also see how easy it is to be complacent.

In the market people make a lot of effort to sell something. *'It was a good day. I was successful in selling ten frying pans.'* Really? Is this the meaning of our life? Selling shoes, selling frying pans, selling our brains, selling whatever we can in order to get food into our mouth and then we die; because we are inside this system which keeps going. *'Don't worry. This is how life is...'*

Some of you might know an old silent film from Fritz Lang called Metropolis. It is an early depiction of what automated mechanical existence is for human beings. The clock determines what we have to do. We fall into line doing what has to be done and there is a lot that has to be done. We are busy. We have a holiday. We buy some new shoes. We get sick and we die. Not such a bad life, but what was it all about?

One of the tragedies in England at the current time is that children, particularly boys, have stopped reading books. It is a profound crisis in education. It seems that the attention span is becoming shorter and shorter, caused, some say, by playing computer games. The first meditation we did this morning was about developing more focussed attention, and we do it by focusing on the breath which is a very boring object. But if you are fourteen years old and you have an Xbox you have excitement moment by moment by moment. You can spend a whole weekend with your friends playing games and getting points with aeroplanes and guns. *'Now I have enough points to buy a helicopter, and with my helicopter I can kill more people and get more points and buy a tank.'* This is a perfect example of samsara. People play these games even into their twenties and thirties. At the end of it all what are they able to do? Press buttons very quickly!

Nuden Dorje is telling us here to be careful since there are many ways to get lost. Thinking that when you die it's all over and so it doesn't matter what we do, is an encouragement to waste our life. Whether karma and rebirth are true or not, as a working hypothesis they support us in the sense of looking beneath the surface. What is it to be alive? I have thoughts but can I trust my thoughts? Who am I? Does life have a meaning? These are the questions that we come close to when we start to study dharma.

Verse 5: Repugnance for Samsara

'The time of your death is uncertain for our life span is like that of a summer flower or a rainbow. The god of death comes as quick as lightning.'

Today the weather is nice, and young people will be out on their motorbikes driving through the hills. There are lots of bends to drive around and when you go round the bend you don't know what's coming the other way. The door to the hospital is open. Today someone in Spain will probably be killed on their motorbike. They went out looking for happiness but death was looking for them. It is a fact that none of us know when we will die. We make all kinds of plans for the future but we don't know if we will be alive or not. When we make plans for the future we are engaging in an exercise of the imagination, and when we are imagining we are not being present.

The encouragement is to think death will come. What is it to be alive here and now, today? What is this life? I see. Who is the one who sees? I hear. Who is the one who hears? I am experiencing. Who is the experiencer? We will have the chance to investigate this in the afternoon.

Verse 6: Taking Refuge

'At that time (of your death) you will find nothing to protect you other than the sole protection of the Guru and the Three Jewels. So you might take refuge six times a day or always in your Guru and the Buddha, Dharma and Sangha.'

The Buddha means your own nature. The Dharma means the truth of our existence: how it is. Sangha here refers to everything that is around you. Taking refuge in the Sangha means 'don't decontextualise yourself'. Our life is other people. How you are is how I can be. In taking refuge in the Sangha we are taking refuge in the sensitivity and malleability required to stay in communication with others; we are opening to movement as movement.

The Buddha is the nature of the mind – the stillness – the unchanging open emptiness The Sangha is the field of experience in which we all move, and the Dharma is the non-duality of these two. Taking refuge in this means relaxing and opening again and again; not living inside our head in some fabricated dream world, but inhabiting our senses and connecting with the shapes and colours.

The body is discontinuous

Towns like Aracena are very attractive however they are full of straight lines. If you walk out of the town you won't find a single straight line since nature is not very fond of straight lines. Human beings impose order, control, and regularity. When you walk along the pavement there is not much danger apart from stepping on dog shit, so you don't have to be very aware. But if you walk on the little path that goes up the hill the stones are unbalanced and if you put your weight down suddenly the stones can shift. Nature is calling you to be aware. So don't go walking in nature absorbed in your thoughts. Don't wander here, thinking about somewhere else. Nature is very special in that way: you have to attend to what is happening. You have to be present. This is what refuge means: being here, present in our senses and working with circumstances. Not taking refuge in ideas *about* things, but coming back again and again to the freshness of embodiment and being connected.

In a city like London very few people are present. Because there are so many people it becomes safe only if you are absent! If you go on the Underground the non-inhabitation of your body is the way to survive. You are completely close to someone, but it is as if they are not there. This is very disconnected and so what Nuden Dorje is encouraging us to do is to observe where you vanish to.

You can vanish into the past with regrets, or you can vanish into the future with fantasies, or you can vanish into your own private domain forgetting the world. These are all kinds of refuge. You are seeking refuge from what is here, whereas actually being here is the best refuge, because if we are fully here then we have access to what we can relate to and engage with.

Taking refuge in the Guru is taking refuge in your own mind; it is not imagining that someone somewhere else is going to protect you and save you. But what is the basis of my existence? Where is my mind? If I have left my mind behind and my mind is the basis of my existence then something is wrong. This is like a five year old child who decides, *'I don't like you and I am not going to live here. I am leaving. I have my doll and some chocolate, and I am leaving!'* But you can't live without your mum.

—*But you won't let me do what I want to do!*

—*That's because I love you.*

When you go off dreaming your own thoughts, where is your mother? Your mind is your mother. You are the child of your mind. Thoughts, feelings, experiences, memories; all of this is the bubbling energy within the womb of the Great Mother. But when we ignore the mother and we cut this root or line to our own ground and become 'I, me, myself,' then we have to hold ourselves together. We have abandoned the mother who never abandons us. From the very beginning the mind is open, empty and infinite. Wherever you go you never leave your mind, but you think you do; you forget your mind, and this is delusion and madness. When he is saying 'take refuge,' it means 'take refuge in the mind itself'. Remember the ground of your being.

You don't have to change the external formation of your life. When we sit in the practice we start to see that this body is experience; sometimes it feels like this and sometimes it feels like that; sometimes I'm aware of my back and sometimes I am not; sometimes I smell something and sometimes not. The body is discontinuous. In our objectified notion of our body we say, *'Of course it's continuous. I have always had this body.'* This is a story. The actuality is you have a discontinuous body; sometimes you have feet and sometimes you don't. If you are sitting here you don't really have functioning feet, but when we get up to go outside then of course we have feet. Life as experience is pulsating, moving, configuring like the clouds appearing and disappearing in the sky. The narrative account of our existence and the direct phenomenology are very different.

Therefore, when we take refuge in the Buddha, Dharma, Sangha and the Guru, we are taking refuge in how it is, and how it is, not what we think it is. How we think it is, is part of how it is, but if we don't approach the world through our thoughts we find it strange. *'Oh, what is this?'* The ego wants to impose order and we do this by editing, by selective attention, by highlighting the things that we like or that appear to be important or that we are afraid of, and we then construct our little picture of our world. But the world is bigger than our picture. All of this – what is it? It is what it is. Yes, but what is it?

There is a fulcrum – a shifting point – when we move from cognitive apprehension to aesthetic appreciation. When you go to the top of the hill and you look out over the valley, the first thing you feel is wow! "Wow!" is enough. 'Wow!' will do very well. *'No, but what is that? Look how the little river goes.'* We chop up the view into bits and now we have our pattern and story. With 'Wow!' we get everything – it is all there. Then we lose this appreciation, the richness, the multiplicity, and start to cut and paste and create the pattern which makes sense to us according to our habitual predilection.

This is what taking refuge means: opening again and again. As we get familiar with this we find there is intrinsic meaning and there is constructed cultural meaning, and that these are not the same. However, cultural meaning is niched within intrinsic meaning as a subset of intrinsic meaning. Intrinsic meaning is the facticity of what is present. It is meaningful because it has ontological significance, not epistemological significance, but without the ontological you wouldn't have the epistemology.

Taking refuge in the Buddha, Dharma, Sangha and the Guru is to open to life moment by moment as it is. This does not mean sitting inside your head looking outside with a telescope, since our self and the world are co-emergent.

Verse 7: The Commitment of Bodhicitta

'All sentient beings in samsara have at one time been your parents, therefore develop bodhicitta of aspiration and practice according to relative and absolute truth. Now that you have gained the excellent support of this human existence, you must practise the undeceiving instructions of your guru.'

Non-duality is embedded in gratitude

The buddhist logic is that all sentient beings have at one time been our parents, and when they were our parents they did many nice things for us. (After Sigmund Freud, parents become very dangerous, but before Freud they were wonderful people who did everything for their children!) Since I have had so many lives, all beings, humans, dogs, cats... have done a lot for me. When I was small and helpless they took care of me and because of that I have a debt of gratitude to each of them. This means that whenever I meet a sentient being there is already a bond between us and a debt of gratitude because we are already connected. There are no real strangers.

This is a wonderful protection against anger, against contempt, against objectification and reification. They have all been our parents. That is to say, they are subjects; they are alive and they have feelings just as we do. We can of course objectify them and wrap them in our judgements, but to see you as a subject I have to look in your eyes and feel you are a real living person. How I am is codetermined by how you are; we are all in this together. All sentient beings are sentient; they are feeling and responding creatures. Therefore, I have to look before I act and my urge to act has to be restrained by my looking.

To cut myself off from you would be to betray myself because part of our dignity as human beings is the quality of gratitude. You have all helped me, so how are you? How you are is significant for me. You can see how this dissolves the bubble of enclosure of 'I, me, myself.' The function of my life is for the other.

In tantric or dzogchen systems they talk about the three kayas or the three aspects of the Buddha. There is the dharmakaya, which is the mind of the Buddha: the formation of the Buddha's awareness. The sambhogakaya, which is the form or the body or the aspect of enjoyment, which in this instance means the fact of experience. And then there is the nirmanakaya, which is the form or the aspect of engagement or participation.

The dharmakaya is for ourselves. When we awaken to our own nature, to this relaxed spacious awareness, we are here, open with whatever happens. What is happening and how this particular embodied form moves within the field of happenstance is for the other, so the sambhogakaya and the nirmanakaya is out towards other people. When we are at home in ourselves and satisfied – not in a smug way but in a relaxed, open way – then there is a lot of energy and availability to be with others.

This also answers the question: What will I do with my life? I will be for the other. None of us can know what that will mean. We have to wait till the other arrives, meaning I will be available. We probably all know what it's like not to be available when we are trapped in pain or the labyrinth of the mind, excitation, anxiety and so on. We are preoccupied and not so available. But when we are relaxed and open it is peaceful and expansive, not preoccupied, and therefore available. How will I be? This is very lovely. I don't know and I don't need to know. I will be as I need to be determined by you.

Traditionally, this is often easier for women to understand than men because usually women spend more time with small children, and to be with small children is to be interrupted. Whatever you think you are going to do, you are not quite going to do it because the child gets sick or forgets something and you have to go back to get it. When you leave the house you ask the child if they need to go to the toilet, and they say they don't, but soon afterwards, in the car on a motorway, the child needs to go.

—*I can't stop here.*

—*But I have to go!*

—*I asked you before we left the house.*

—*I am sorry, Mamma. I didn't know.*

This is life. To be for the other is to be interrupted; it means not going in a straight line. It means responding to circumstances. If you have invested a lot in your plan, your idea, or your map, then this is a nuisance and so annoying. The map is irrelevant; the fact is, we need to do something.

The disturbance is not a disturbance – it is life – and to be in life means to go where life takes us. This is freedom from the will to power; this is anti-totalitarian.

As far as we know, Mae Tse Tung and Joseph Stalin did not spend much time wiping babies' bottoms. They were doing much more important things like establishing the Gulag, killing their enemies, implementing a five-year plan to help over ten million people die of starvation.

—*This plan must not be disturbed and anyone who objects to the five-year plan is an enemy of the revolution and should die.*

—*But El Presidente I need to go pee pee!*

—*Stop the revolution – we have pee pee!*

We can see that softness, gentleness and malleability is the real power of connectivity: staying connected however the circumstances arise. So when we have this idea that all beings have been our parents in previous lives this is a kind of supportive metaphor or idea to allow us to transcend the limitation of this eternal cry, "But what about me?"

Then he says that **on the basis of this we should develop the relative and absolute truth qualities of the bodhicitta or the bodhisattva orientation of working for the liberation of all beings.**

On the relative truth level, it means, "*I will help you.*" This is still operating within the paradigm of the Three Wheels: the self, the other, and the connection between them. It is also very important and helpful: "*I am for you.*" However in the absolute truth formation it means, "*Who are you? Who am I and what does it mean to help you?*" Your nature from the very beginning is open awareness, and my nature is also this ever-present awareness, so you already have what you need so I will help you by giving you what you already have. How do we help other people awaken? This will depend on the person. If we see the person as fixed or limited we have to unscrew some of these limiting factors. If we see them as patterns of energy then we have to get into the rhythm of the energy. Just as in the school playground if two girls are holding a skipping rope and turning it, and one girl is jumping with the rope, if you want to join her then you have to get your body into the rhythm of the rope and you jump in and join her in the movement. You don't impose your rhythm. It is by being available into how things are that we find other people, and that's easier if we see that how they are is just a rhythm, a pattern, a vibration.

From the deep absolute point of view, everything has been empty from the very beginning. There is no truth to the limitation; it has as much truth as a rainbow or a mirage. Within that open state everything is already awakened and so when we connect with other beings there is no judgment. They are as they are; it is as it is; this is how it is. We don't need to think, *'Oh, it would be better if we did...'* What is there to improve?

This is called the absolute truth bodhicitta, which is full of respect with whatever formation arises but sees it as appearance and emptiness. Therefore, we are validating the vitality of the other without being pulled into the fantasy that they truly exist as someone. You have a full meeting and contact but without solidification.

He goes on to say, **'Now that you have gained the excellent support of this human existence, you must practise the undeceiving instructions of your guru.'** The word guru is quite problematic in many European cultures as it can speak of a kind of sect formation: of somebody who has an esoteric or secret knowledge which they only give out to other people according to certain conditions. However the meaning of the word 'guru' here is the one who helps you to be a learner. The focus is not on teaching but on learning.

Hopefully, when we meet together like this you become more curious about yourself. Not just about why you have certain thoughts, but where do these thoughts come from? Who is the one who has the thought? This is the function of trying to facilitate the way of attending to things as they are.

The instruction of the guru is not that you should go and do something, but that you should hang out with yourself, be close to yourself, and be supportive and friendly of yourself. Not judging or trying to change yourself, but simply observing these patterns as they arise and pass. Then we notice the tendencies we have. Everybody has tendencies and we each have our own particular patterning. Who is the one who reveals the tendencies?

The answer to our problems doesn't lie in improving the quality of the contents of our mind, although that's not a bad thing to do and that would be useful in making us more helpful for other people.

There are many things about the world I don't know. For instance, I don't know anything about car engines, so if your car breaks down I can't help you. If I knew about car engines it would make me more helpful as a person in certain situations. Whatever we learn, whether it's sewing, dancing, singing or knitting, these can be useful in certain areas, but they are all relative. The key thing is for us to learn about ourselves. This doesn't mean developing a narcissistic orientation, but to see how I am? What is the ground of my being, and what is the patterning of my becoming?

Following the instruction of the teacher means to turn your gaze toward yourself. To become calm and clear. To be honest in the seeing of limiting patterns. To allow them to be there, neither pushing them away nor merging into them. In that way we learn for ourselves the self-liberating nature of the mind.

Of course you can read about all this in books, but that only gives you an idea about an idea. Only by being with yourself and by observing your own mind will you see that this is what impermanence tastes like – this is how it is. And that means following the instructions. It is not about being a clone, or a student of someone; the key thing is **to be a student of yourself**. Observe how you open and how you close. What is the effect of the full moon on you? What is the effect of the seasons? What is the effect of being in these hills, or being by the sea, or being in a village or a city?

'I am different in different situations.' 'I am unreliable and unpredictable.' If you see this then were you still at school you would get a gold star! *'Well done! Great news! You are unreliable. You don't know how you are going to be. This is fantastic because last week you knew exactly what everything was! Last week I couldn't get inside you but now you don't know, I can meet you because you have some gaps, some space, and some curiosity.'*

This is the way we want to approach the situation.

Verse 8: Awareness, karma and virtuous action

'You must be careful to discriminate without error between the virtuous actions that are to be adopted, and the non-virtuous actions which are to be abandoned. You yourself will experience the consequences of your bad actions.'

On the level of emptiness it is the same: on the level of compassion it is not the same

The fact that everything is like an illusion – there, but not there – like the reflection of a full moon on a pond, doesn't mean that everything is just the same. Helping people and harming people is not the same. On the level of emptiness it is the same; on the level of compassion it is not the same. If you sit in the house of wisdom and forget compassion you become a demon. 'Everything is empty so it doesn't matter, and I can do as I like' This is a very wrong view.

On one level of course it is true; everything is just like a mirage, but some parts of the mirage have a smiley face and other bits have a sad face. Would you like to have a sad or a happy face? Hands up for the happy face! We all know being kind to people, being connected with them, and thinking about them makes them come alive. On one level it doesn't matter and yet it does matter. But if it matters too much or if it's too real then we become helpless.

At this time across the world there are small babies being raped. There are young girls having clitoridectomies with a broken piece of glass. There are so many bad things; what shall we do with this? This is real: this is not real. How shall we live in a world full of suffering? The Buddha recommends 'The Middle Way'. If you make it too real you become overwhelmed and can't do anything. If you go to the other extreme and you desensitise yourself so that nothing impacts you, you become useless. 'The Middle Way' means we respond and have empathic attunement without being overwhelmed.

To say, *'Oh, these things happen.'* doesn't mean that the heart has become a stone. It is not a statement of indifference but it is a fact that these things happen. Therefore we want to find an effective way of bringing about change. Just going to someone else's country and telling them that they are wrong is probably not very helpful, because really what you are saying is that my belief is better than yours. This is not likely to make most people feel prepared to change.

Through meditation we come to understand how our own beliefs and attachments are operating, and so when we encounter such extremist totalitarian mental states in others we realise this is just an extreme form of the way our own mind operates. I can also get locked into a 'good versus bad,' 'right versus wrong' frame of mind. Compassion means being available to the situation as it is and working with the limitations of others without telling them that they are bad. Paradoxically, the more we understand and see how easy it is to get lost then the kinder and more tuned in we can be to other people who get very lost. Being aware of the difference between good and bad, helpful and unhelpful, means being very attentive to the precise details of the situation.

In the tradition it says that your wisdom should be as vast as the sky and your compassion should be as fine as the point of a needle. This is because compassion is about the detail, about the actuality of how someone else is. Setting out codes of conduct and moral rules is very easy, but working with people in the actual complexity of their lives is more difficult because we don't know what to do. It is not about mastery. The master musician knows how to play the notes before the concert begins, but when we meet other people we don't know what to say. We find our way; a way which is always fresh and which emerges through openness and being with the other.

Verse 9: The terrifying experience of death

'Yama, the terrifying god of death knows all the good and bad things you have done. Wherever you are born you will only experience misery and suffering. Other than the Three Jewels you will find no refuge to protect you or to accompany you.'

The Four aspects of karma

It means you can't get away with it. There are countries in the world where you can open a secret bank account and as long as the police don't catch you, you get away with it. Many criminals get away with it and never go to court, but they have the karma.

Karma is a very important term and there are four aspects to karma. The first aspect is called the foundation or basis. It represents dualism: If I exist and you exist there is a field of potential between us: you have money that I want to get from you, or you have some suffering that I want to help you with.

The second level is intention: I have an intention towards you, maybe to help you or maybe to harm you.

The third aspect is the actual connection in which I carry out the deed. For example, I go to visit you in the hospital or I take your purse when you are not looking. It is enacted through the body.

The fourth aspect is the conclusion: I have cheated you and I am glad, or I have managed to help you a little bit and I am pleased. It means that you align yourself fully with what you have done. Maybe you go to hospital for many weeks to help this person. You are sitting with them as they are dying saying some prayers and mantras. Their family never come to see them, but you are there for them and they die. After some weeks the lawyer reads the will and all the money has gone to the relatives. *'The fucking bastard! I was in the hospital all the time. What a bloody waste of time!'* This thought, this disavowal of what one has done, can reverse the incipient karma. You are now unhappy that you did this virtuous action. It often happens that people are inside some vision trying to be a good person, and at a certain point they think, *'Oh, you are taking the piss! What is this?'*

For meditators, the most important part here is the first point: the belief that subject and object are separate and real. This is the world as revealed through ignorance. When you are inside this, you are necessarily going to be pulled into intentions towards the other. The way out of karma is to relax the investment in subject and object as strongly real and to see them as two waves moving on the surface of the ocean. For as long as we are living as an individual subject we are like the cover of a book: some mark can be made on it. When we relax into the openness of the mind it is like the mirror. The mirror shows everything but is not marked by it, but the ego as a thing is marked and shaped by whatever it encounters. As long as we sit inside this self-formation and we think it's the whole truth about who we are, we are going to be impacted by events.

Yama, the lord of death, is supposed to see our 'report card' when we die and decide where we are going to go.

'Wherever you are born you will experience only misery and suffering. Other than the Three Jewels you will find no refuge to protect you and accompany you.'

Dharma is supposed to protect us from fear, but in order to protect you from fear it firstly has to make sure you are really afraid.

—*Don't be a bad girl. You know what happens to bad girls – not good news.*

—*I want to be a good girl.*

When you look around the world it's frightening. Not only would it be scary for us to be in many situations but we couldn't help ourselves let alone help other people.

If we want to fulfil the idea of the bodhisattva and really be available for other people we can only do this from a position of freedom. Every time we engage in a strongly invested activity and give ourselves into something small, this over-investment leads to an inability to see the wider field.

For example, in the hospital department that I was in charge of it was quite a small world but it ran well. I had to do many activities to maintain some autonomy and a capacity to fulfil our vision of how we wanted it to be. However, when I announced that I was going to retire, the manager above me said, *'Oh, we don't need someone like you again. We will get someone with fewer qualifications. We can pay them less money and life will still go on.'* My beautiful structure collapsed in the dust. It seemed important to me at the time, but it was always going to be destroyed. Although I have been studying buddhism for a long time, unfortunately this has not protected me from stupidity! I wanted to draw my sword and be a brave hero fighting for this hospital unit, but in the end all heroes lie in the grave.

This is the fantasy that Nuden Dorje is pointing to here. Keep the panoramic vision. Don't get caught by the over-investment of one small fantasy. Ignorance is decontextualisation. The ego is the energy of the open mind, but an energy which decides bloody-mindedly to forget its own root. Contextualisation – being part of the field of experience – is really important and this is the best protection against being caught in the waves of karma.

No kind of worldly success will provide enduring protection; not money; not health; not good colleagues; not loving children. Eventually we die and go alone. Remember that when you lie on your deathbed people may be smiling at you full of love, but it is you who are dying, not them. After they put you in the ground, they don't pluck out their eyes; they go and eat and drink.

—*Oh, what a good man.*

—*Oh yes, he was really great.*

Munch, munch... Chomping away on their food! You go alone. All that is here will vanish. The real context is the infinity of the mind, not this particular zeitgeist: not this particular moment of space and time, this mood, or the cultural issues about the economy or the war or whatever.

Verse 10: The Living Experience of the Guru

'The embodiment of all the Buddhas of the past, present and future is your root guru, the one who has all qualities and shows you the threefold kindness of giving you material support, dharma teachings and enlightenment. So you should keep him at all times on the crown of your head with ceaseless remembrance. To meet such a guru is as hard as for flowers to appear in the sky. To receive his teaching is as rare as the appearance of stars in the daytime. Therefore you should pray that you merge inseparably with his mind.'

The Buddhas of the past are gone. The Buddhas of the present haven't come. They certainly haven't come here – maybe they have come somewhere else. We don't know if the Buddhas of the future are coming or not. What we have is being here together, so how can we find the optimal value in this situation? By opening ourselves to the possibility of learning something new.

There was a song in the 1960's *'If you can't be with the one you love, love the one you're with'*. If we can't find Padmasambhava, at least we have Mr Low here for a while *[laughter]* because valuing what is in the palm of your hand is useful. I try to be open and transparent with you. I probably don't see myself as clearly as you see me, but my faults and limitations and obsessions are probably obvious. Our concern is with workability.

In tantra there is a lot about the idealisation of the guru, but what can you do with something very idealised? In England we have a queen who sits on a throne. She wears a crown and has a fairytale carriage to travel in, but I have personally never met her. She has nothing to do with me. I know some people and I talk with and work with them. They don't have a palace or a throne, but at least if I say hello they say hello back. This is the meaning of life – from activity not idealisation.

Idealisation makes us small. From my own experience in going to work every day there is no point in being the size of a peanut. You have to value yourself if you are going to overcome the difficulties of each day.

Opening up these ideas means being respectful to the qualities of other people is important. If you think only one person is perfect and can help you, then how often are you going to see them? Not very often. But when you start to respect everyone you meet, see how many allies you have!

Just watching the different children playing in the square here you see human psychology in operation. You see selfishness in the one child who is always grabbing the ball and running away with it. You see collaboration and kindness. They are showing you what is helpful and what is unhelpful. They remind us to be more thoughtful. If we learn how to learn then truly the whole world becomes the guru.

We hear the leaves rustling together when the wind blows through them. How fragile our life is. The leaf, which is quite big, is attached by a narrow stalk to the tree. What is the line connecting me with my life? I can die. What am I doing? Who am I? Everyone can be your ally and this is then a really wonderful world and you can practise dharma all the time; it is not some special activity you do sitting on a cushion.

'You should keep the guru at all times on the crown of your head with ceaseless remembrance. To meet such a guru is as hard as for flowers to appear in the sky. To receive his teaching is as rare as the appearance of stars in the daytime.'

He is telling us to take the dharma as something very precious. Don't put it away in a box, but keep the teacher on the crown of your head. This is a nice Asian idea that the top of your head is a holy place. We want the guru in our skin. We want the teaching and the meditation practice to flow through us all the time. How do we do that? By seeing it how it is, not by seeing it as something esoteric and special since it will then be in contradiction to ordinary life. Whether you are making a cup of tea, or going to the toilet, or talking to a friend, all of these are experiences arising in the mirror of the mind. There is no experience outside of emptiness. The guru is the presence of emptiness.

Having devotion to the guru means offering everything to the guru, so we offer everything into space. The sound of a car is the sound of emptiness. Sitting in the restaurant talking and laughing together is the sound of emptiness. The pure sound of dharma. Dharma is everywhere.

'Therefore you should pray that you merge inseparably with his mind.'

What is the mind of the guru? It is space. It is the dharmakaya. Everything we do here together is moving in the space of the mind... arising and passing...and this itself is liberation. There is nothing to be done but to allow the self-liberation of all phenomena and through this we come to see the self-perfecting nature of the mind.

The next couple of verses are also setting the context. We might wonder where is dzogchen in all of these general dharma ideas? But the context is important because it is how we open ourselves.

In Verse 7 we were told that we should have gratitude to all beings because they have been our parents in previous lives. Now we are told that we should have gratitude to our teacher. What is the meaning of gratitude? Gratitude means 'thank you'. I appreciate how you are and how that is for me. Essentially it means that I wouldn't be me without you; it is you who allow me to be me.

THE SEA OF LANGUAGE

If our parents didn't speak to us when we were very small, the opportunity to enter the world of language would close. There are reports from various countries and at various times of children who were found running wild. They learnt to survive by running and hunting with dogs or wolves, but they couldn't speak and it was very difficult for them to learn to speak. The fact that we can speak is based on the fact of parents and friends talking with us; without them we would be empty; we are filled with them and this is amazing.

Gratitude starts to dissolve the barrier of duality; without you there is no me. *'I am me because I am not you!'* is our ordinary ego position: I am who I am. But what do we have? Language. We were invited into it by people repeatedly speaking to us when we were small, and kindly correcting our grammar and vocabulary. The teachers at school helped us to learn to read and write and not to make our notebooks such a mess. The competencies that we now have were transmitted to us; we become ourselves through the other.

What then is this separation of myself? This is a really important question. If you speak Spanish this is because you are in the sea of Spanish and like a fish swimming in the sea you swim in this sea of language. If the fish comes out of the sea it starts to die. Your sense of self and your capacity to think and make sense of your world is because you can swim in a language that was here before you were born. But we feel we own our language. However my independence is dependent on the kindness of others.

Many children find this fact very painful and humiliating to have to recognise: that you couldn't be a teenager going out in the world without the kindness of your parents. *'You can't tell me what to do!*

Leave me alone! I am myself.' This is nothing but madness. The teenager has become themselves because someone put food on the table and someone helped them pack their school bag etc. That is why the view of non-duality is embedded in gratitude. Gratitude is not an optional quality like some aspect of our personality that it would be nice to develop a bit more of; it is absolutely fundamental.

In buddhism we learn about mudras, different gestures that are an important part of learning. I would like us all now to practise the mudra of life. Please take your right hand and bring it over your mouth. Now squeeze your nostrils. *[laughter]* Your life is breathing. So, gratitude. Without this world coming into us we die. The other is ourself. This is not theory; this is life itself. Drinking, eating, pissing, shitting is the cycle of existence. Gratitude to parents, to authors, to filmmakers, to clothes makers... Everything is given to us and this is how we participate in life. We give and we receive; breathing out and breathing in, speaking and listening... Subject and object weaving the world together. Not two separate domains or self-existing things, but a ceaseless flow of co-emergence.

Seeing this is the basis for practising dzogchen. Seeing that I am energy moving in a sea of energy. Seeing that I am strong and fragile. Seeing that I am open and closed, as are other people. So how shall we bring our energy in contact with the energy of others? This brings us back, again and again, to the ground of emergence. With that basis we start to be able to look at our own minds.

But before that Nuden Dorje gives a short praise to the instructions which will then follow.

Verse 11 and 12: Buddhahood in our Hand

'All the Buddhas of the past, present and future travel the path of these teachings and now you are fortunate to have met this secret path. The heart essence of all the Buddhas is just this and nothing else, the secret certain essence of Ati Dzogpa Chenpo.'

There are many different kinds of buddhist teachings on architecture, on how to build monasteries and make statues, on how to do visualisation practices and on how to lay out an altar in the correct manner. You can learn all these things. They are a kind of syllabus and very useful.

The Incredible String Band, a Scottish band, have a song with the lines,

> "Oh, you know all the words, and you sung all the notes
> But you never quite learned the song"

You can know a lot about dharma. You can memorise dharma texts. These are the words, but what is the tune? What is the living flow that links it all together? This is your own mind – your own clarity – your own awareness. And it is the heart of dzogpa chenpo.

Verse 12: 'If you gain an irreversible realisation of this teaching then you gain the understanding of a Buddha. Hard to really understand it is like a wish-fulfilling jewel. You must practice the wisdoms of listening, reflecting and meditation diligently and without sloppiness.'

Are Buddhas Allowed to be Sad?

We can imagine that the Buddha is very bright and shiny living in a beautiful buddha realm with no problems. Why wouldn't the Buddha have problems? The Buddha promises to help everybody. If I am with you then your problems become my problems, but the Buddha has problems the way the mirror has reflections. The reflection is in the mirror, but it doesn't touch the mirror. The Buddha has problems, has compassion and feelings for all beings, but he is not mixed up or contaminated by this. We can learn from this.

When we meditate, the presence of all kinds of thoughts which might seem difficult or bad doesn't mean that we need to do some other kind of practice. The thoughts are in the mind and the mind is open. The mind is Buddha. All kinds of things arise and don't stop your mind being Buddha if you simply allow them to be there.

One of the ways that people misunderstand the meaning of Buddha is to wrap him in some idealising fantasy: 'He is different from you and you must try very hard to be like him.' Wait a minute...this is very bad...the Buddha is not like you. What about non-duality? That doesn't mean the Buddha is the same as you, or you are the same as the Buddha. It means, don't put the Buddha up on a pedestal and put yourself down as an ordinary person. The Buddha is your own mind pure from the very beginning and this space can incorporate everything. Everything is already integrated within this mind so it is not about keeping the good and the bad separate. The good and the bad have no essence or substance; they are the ceaseless play of the clarity of the mind.

If you don't understand this point, and you keep thinking, *'Well I am not like the Buddha because the Buddha is wonderful. I get sad. The Buddha can't be sad because he's so wonderful.'* Who says? Is there a Public Relations Department producing endless brochures and shiny pictures of a 'Happy Buddha'? But why do you want to limit the

Buddha to just being happy? Are Buddhas not allowed to be sad? Why? This is prejudice. We are standing up for the rights of Buddhas to be sad! This is very important in the buddhist understanding because at the very beginning of this text we have a verse which starts: MA CHOE TROE DRAL LA MA CHOE KYI KU. The second two words 'TROE DRAL' mean that the dharmakaya mind of the Buddha is free of binary opposition: it is not held within any of our usual polarising categories. To say that the Buddha is always happy and never sad is a polarity.

When you sit in meditation, relaxed and open, everything arises, all of samsara and all of nirvana. Everything is contained within the spacious mind. Is this the Buddha? You can read many dzogchen texts which say that your own mind is the Buddha. This doesn't mean that your ego formation or your sense of self is the Buddha. Rather, with n the openness of your awareness there is space for your ego, and the qualities which are arising there are held inside the infinite clarity of the mind.

When it says the Buddha is free of suffering, we have to understand what 'free from' means. If we have Buddha here and suffering over there with a gap in the middle then it becomes easy to see. *'Oh yes, suffering here – Buddha there – that makes sense.'* But the mirror has a reflection of a pile of dog shit and this reflection is inside the mirror. The mirror is free of the reflection of dog shit although the dog shit reflection is inside the mirror. This is why the image of the mirror is very important in dzogchen.

'Free of', or 'without' doesn't mean pushed apart; it means that the primordial untouchable purity of the mind, which is referred to as vajra or indestructible, is there no matter whatever arises. The Buddha is not determined by the content of the mind, so endlessly trying to purify the content of your mind is not the main activity of our practice. Instead, we want to relax and open to the infinity of the mind itself and that state is free of all limitations whatever arises.

This is the ending of the first introductory part, and after the break we will go into the mind itself.

Break

Verse 13: Looking for the Nature of the Mind

'Your own mind is the root of all phenomena. When you first start to practise the word 'mind' sounds very big. Where does mind come from, where does it rest and where does it go? What shape is it and what colour does it have? By enquiring into the shape of your mind you must again and again come to a definite understanding of its real nature.'

The Mind is the Illuminator

Your own mind is the root of all phenomena. The word 'mind' here indicates your basic capacity to know, rather than its more familiar usage to indicate the totality of your thoughts, feelings, sensations and so on. In the ordinary sense, the dualistic sense, my mind exists in relation to the things it knows. However here Nuden Dorje is not saying that your mind exists in relation to all phenomena, but that it is the actual root of all that you experience. Without this root you would have no experience. That is to say, there are no things out-with your mind.

There is the famous question in Indian philosophy: *If a tree falls in a forest and nobody hears it falling does it make a sound?* Is sound an object which just is — a some thing — or is it an experience? Without someone to experience it, what is sound? Sound arises as sound with the hearer. That is the sense in which it is said that the mind that gives birth to all phenomena including sound. You could imagine something, but who is doing the imagining? Our mind. Whether it makes a sound or not we may have our opinions on this, but this again is our mind. The mind is implicated in everything that occurs; without the mind there is just nothing at all because the mind shows the presence of whatever it is.

You might think that if you have a torch on a dark night and if you shine the torch around you see different things; as if the things illuminated by the torch were there, but in a kind of form, until awakened or revealed by the light of the torch. That would be our usual way of thinking about things. But actually what he is saying here is that the mind is the field of clarity within which things appear. They don't appear *to* the mind, they appear *within* the mind. If they appeared to the mind – mind is here – the arising object is here – and when the arising object gets nearer the mind goes, *'Oh! There you are.'* Object and subject. But the mind is not the subject.

'I see the green pillar.' This is true. 'I,' the subject, sees the green pillar. My mind is illuminating the facticity of the green pillar. But while I have a sense that 'I' see the pillar – 'I see the' – is self-illuminating. As I illuminate the pillar, I illuminate myself, so what is the ground of the illumination? This is the mind. 'I see the pillar' is the subject form arising in, to, and for the mind. The green pillar is the object form arising in, to, and for the mind. Subject and object appear to be separate, but having the same ground and the same field of manifesting, they are inseparable.

Here you have the double non-duality: subject and object are non-dual because they always arise together, and this non-dual form of subject and object is itself non-dual from its own ground just as the reflection is in the mirror. The reflection could be a complex reflection such as two people looking at each other. In terms of the reflection of the two people these reflections are in the same plane of reflection and are not two entities each having their own essence and substance yet simultaneously inseparable from the mirror. You cannot take a reflection out of a mirror. You can't take a thought out of the mind. The life of the mind is thoughts, feelings and sensations.

All phenomena – whether experienced as subject or object, in any place or at any time – are rooted in your own mind. It doesn't go out of your mind, nor is it exactly synonymous with your mind, but it is rooted in the mind and it is what the mind shows.

'When you first start to practise the word 'mind 'sounds very big.' People talk about the nature of the mind and sometimes give this a capital 'M' meaning the Big Important Mind, but it is also just our mind. Nevertheless, our mind is not whatever we think it is since the mind cannot be caught by thought.

It is possible when a child is small for the mother to know almost everything about the child, but it's never possible for the child to know everything about the mother. The mind is the mother. Our mind is not what we think it is. The thought is the child of the mind mother, so when we think about ourselves we can't actually catch the mind mother. Thoughts can catch thoughts. Somebody says something and we reply, *'I need to think about that. I'll get back to you. I'll look in my diary to see if that's possible and if I have time.'* The proposal is there as an idea and you run other ideas around that idea and you are able to come to a conclusion. *'Yes, that's a good idea.'* or *'No, I don't think so.'* In that way, one idea catches the other idea, but an idea cannot catch the mind itself, This is what Nuden Dorje is describing here.

How and why we question the mind

Some of these very important questions you will know: **'Where does the mind come from? Where does it rest and where does it go?'** asks us to think about how in the moment when your mind seems to be here, where is it and where does it go to? **'What shape is it and what colour does it have?"**

'By enquiring into the root of your mind you must again and again come to a definite understanding of its real nature or its true nature.' He is saying if you want to open to how your existence actually is, don't rely on speculation. Don't pump out a whole stream of ideas of maybe it's this or maybe it's that, otherwise you will just have thought production. All of us have already had millions of thoughts in this life, so we can be sure of one thing about thoughts:

they go. A transient thought is not going to give you the mind which is unchanging. That is why it is very important how we take up these questions.

We might ask ourselves, 'Where does my hand come from?' My hand seems to grow out of my arm. Where does it stay? It stays on the end of my arm. Where does it go? It doesn't go anywhere; it is always stuck on the end of my arm. This account is not difficult to understand because I can look and see my hand. The relation between my hand and my arm seems obvious.

However the relation between the thoughts and feelings arising in the mind and the mind itself is not so obvious. Although experience shows or displays the energy or potential of the mind, the specificity of these experiences does not show you the actual mind itself. A reflection doesn't show you the mirror itself; it shows you the mirror's potential to display an image of something outside the mirror. However indirectly, by inference, a reflection shows you the essence of the mirror for it is the mirror's empty ungraspable indefinability that is the basis for the display of the reflection.

When we go back into the meditation, maybe what is arising is an awareness of tension in the body or you might hear a sound that you take to be a car outside. We are sitting with our gaze open so we see colours and shapes – some thoughts and feelings are arising – and these are registered because of the mind. In the moment of the arising of this experience, where is the mind? Did the mind come to be here in order to show the experience?

For example, you hear a sound, *'Oh, there's a car going by outside.'* It is as if my mind is going out there. My thought is going there and it is as if my hearing is going there, but is my mind going there? Does the mind go from here to there? It is your mind. This is your work and nobody can do it for you. If we go to eat together and I take my knife and fork and eat what is on your plate, you will not be satisfied; you have to eat what is on your own plate. You each have your own mind with your own set of tendencies and memories and this is the jungle of your own existence. Many things happen at once and you know it because you have a mind.

As far as we know the cup on my table is not troubled by thoughts and feelings. We don't say that the cup is a sentient being, since it doesn't have a mind. We register the cup, but the cup doesn't register us. Something is happening – we know it is happening – the knower is here. Where is this knower? Is it big or small? Is it inside your body, inside your head, or is it outside? Does it have a particular shape or colour?

These are important questions because generally speaking we can answer these questions about any object in the world. I can tell what the shape and colour of my spectacles are and I know that I bought them in a chemist shop. The pair that I had before got broken, so probably after some time these will also get broken and end up in the dustbin. They came from a shop and now they are in my hand, but in the future they will go in a dustbin. We can answer similar questions about the chair – our shoes – the trees – everything. These are the questions that are used to establish the identity of something.

When people arrive on the coast of Greece in a little rubber boat, they are taken to a reception centre. They are asked where they have come from and where do they want to go? The Greeks then decide whether a person can stay or not. They take a photo of them and a thumbprint. They establish their weight, colour, shape and height, and from this they work out if this person is an illegal immigrant, an economic migrant, or a genuine refugee. We use these questions all the time to establish identity, and this sense of identity is reified to give us the sense there is something knowable there.

Is the mind also a phenomenon then? In the first sentence of this verse he says that all dharma and phenomena have their root in the mind. We know that we can answer these five questions about phenomena, which is why these questions are important. Because if you can fit your mind into these five questions then the mind is a normal thing like every other normal thing. But when we look, again and again, it becomes clear that we can't fit the mind into these questions. We then see that the mind is other than everything else.

The movement of the mind is the patterning of all phenomena. The movement is inseparable from the mind, but the mind is not like its own movement. The movement has shape, colour, position and location; it is relative and stands in relation to something else. The jug is bigger than the glass. We see one thing and then we see another thing and we compare and contrast. The thingness of the thing is established by its relation with other things. Or to put it another way, all finites stand in relation to other finites. But what does the infinite stand in relation to? The finite has an edge or a boundary. This glass comes to an end because it won't go into the jug; when the finites meet together they have a boundary which is mutually excluding.

But is the mind infinite? If it fits in these five questions it is finite and if it doesn't fit in these five questions it is infinite; so these questions are very important. Each of us has to examine them for ourselves because this is our own existence.

We are not talking about some thing out there. We are here and our being here-ness is our life. I am alive: I think, I feel, I see. This is the mind. The mind shows this; it's not theory. So what is in my mind? If we don't know this we are just telling story about story and there is no end to stories. We are trapped in the dimension of arising and passing phenomena. We are trapped in the domain of the reflection which has no way of being in touch with the mirror from which it is inseparable. I am here because of my mind. I can say with confidence 'I am here,' but what is the mind?

We will now do a short meditation practice. When we sit we relax and open and then just allow these questions to emerge in the mind. We want to allow the mind to show itself even though it is not something that can be shown. If you go actively looking, that very orientation will make it impossible to find. If you go into the forest looking for a deer you don't crash about through the bushes, because as soon as the deer hears this it will run away. You go in very quietly and then you sit quietly, and if you are fortunate the deer will wander out through the forest. You are not actively looking, but you are present, and that non-disturbing presence allows the sense of the mind to reveal itself.

Sitting practice

KNOWING BY BEING

We want to take up these questions in a very gentle way. Our normal sense of knowledge is something which apprehends and takes hold of the thing that it knows, but if the mind cannot be apprehended then how can we know it? It's a knowing by being.

We are open and in that openness there is no limit. It is a self-proving knowing which is self-validating without being self-reflexive; it doesn't confirm itself as there is nothing firm – it is just there. It is like relaxing into the state of presence.

In the tradition we take up these questions again and again. Some people even have them as their main practice for years and years because they are ways of sloughing off the formation of conclusions and open the space for 'just this'. This is a mystery as it doesn't fit inside the interpretive matrix within which we ordinarily function, but that doesn't mean that it's a fantasy. On the contrary it is very precise, very clear and just here. It is the opposite of confusion. The fact that one can't say exactly what it is, is because of the limit of language. We can give lots of examples, but we can't define it in words.

The traditional Tibetan example for this is when somebody doesn't know the meaning of the term 'sweet.' You can try to describe what this is or you can just put a small spoon of honey on their tongue.

—*Oh, that is sweet!*

—*You know now. Okay, so tell me what it's like?*

—*I can't.*

This is how transmission is in dzogchen. We want to create the circumstances where you find yourself 'tasting' and being diffused by this quality of openness. Talking about it may help give some sense of the frame but ultimately it cannot be described.

What does help of course is the ongoing work of experiencing yourself as part of this unfolding picture. When you go outside and you are walking you can experience that from inside the frame of 'I am walking,' or you can experience the revelation of walking. When you come to the door you push it open and you step out. You push the door because it's the kind of door that opens when you push it. The door shows you what to do. You come to the top of the stairs. The stair says, *'Please bend your knee'*, so you bend your knee and you go down the stairs. It's amazing! Now, *'Bend the other knee.'* Each step shows you what to do. Now you are on the pavement, so you don't need to bend your knees like that or you will look pretty stupid. Now you are walking and you come to cross the road. You look and listen for any cars. To be present is to be part of this world. It is not, 'I am walking,' or 'I am going down the stairs,' as if I am conquering Mount Everest. It is not heroic; it is not a struggle; it is working with the nature of the stairs or the nature of the pavement.

You come to a place to eat and you sit down. How you sit down depends on the height of the seat and the strength of the muscles in your legs, and the balance of the weight in your torso. If you are with your self you can sit down: I am part of this. I am not acting *on* the world; I am acting *with* the world. The world and I are on this great stage and each shape of the world calls me into my shape. A knife and a fork may be very important but not if you have soup. You pick up the spoon for the soup. You just observe, *'I am responding in the world as part of the world'* and the fruit for us as meditators is that it shows us the dynamic unfolding nature of what is going on. This is the direct experience of non-duality. It is not something strange or abstract or mystical; it is the attunement that we have with the world as part of the interactive flow of experience.

The more we experience ourselves as this co-emergent energy or experience, the easier it is to open to the mind itself. But when we sit in identification with our thoughts, reifying and solidifying the phenomena around us, then it is more difficult. So the practice is allowing our inseparability from the environment with everything we do.

Day Three

RELEASE OURSELVES FROM THE SPELL OF THOUGHT AND LANGUAGE

Time goes by. We have today and tomorrow morning left, so we want to use the time well to address the central issues.

In the Bible both Genesis and the Gospel of John highlight the nature of naming. Genesis describes how God creates the world and then names each thing in it. The Gospel of John says, *'In the beginning was the Word.'* The Logos. Logos is not just a word but a whole force of organisation. *'And the Word was with God, and the Word was God.'* This is very powerful as it speaks of the magical nature of language – things are called into being by naming.

For example, certain nomenclature is very dangerous. Some hundreds of years ago very easy to name a woman as a witch and it could lead to torture and burning. Once a word is stuck on to someone it is very difficult to take it off. We even say, 'There is no smoke without fire.' Once an identification or naming is put on to someone we think there must be a reason for it, and then we look to the object. We investigate the object and see, *'Ah yes, you are really a witch.'* rather than thinking, *'Maybe the person who said they were a witch is up to some funny business.'*

We know that for small children it is very important for them to learn to use language and be able to tell the world what it is. We are living in the middle point between two forces: one is that the world shows me what it is, and the other is that I tell the world what it is. When children are about two years old they are not very much in language and so they experience the world showing them how the world is. Taking a child of that age out for a walk is very slow because they are surprised by so many things they see. The world is showing them wonders. The mind is still fresh. A few years later they are projecting their own ideas out onto the world, and this power to name things and to shape them according to their mental structures becomes a source of ego identity and functional power.

We could say that the key function of meditation is to try to rectify this imbalance. We are too active in telling the world and ourselves what is going on. In English we say, *'Look before you leap'*, but we also need to look before we speak. What is there? Then we respond. If we are full of words then the words bubble out and the world is then full of words. Sometimes there is nothing but words, and then we are tied up in this endless matrix of wordy thought construction. Thoughts can be useful when they are used for a clear purpose, but they have a tendency to take on a life of their own.

A great deal of our mental activity is like tinnitus. There are different ideas about what causes tinnitus. One is that these very fine hair-like tentacles that are inside the ear and which vibrate in response to vibrations of the air, become bored of being the servant. They wait around all day long and then some vibration comes along and they have to dance – so they decide they can dance by themselves! People who have tinnitus hear sounds going on all the time. It doesn't mean anything, but it can be a cause of great disturbance. Our thoughts are like that. We can have so many thoughts but they don't do any useful work; they take on a life of their own and they reinforce each other. We have all had the experience of being worried about something and seeing how thoughts feed upon thoughts. We keep chewing on the same issue like a dog with an old bone; there is nothing to be gained but we keep chewing because it becomes an automated function.

Reframe the Thought as Irrelevant

In order to do the practice we need to release ourselves from the spell of thought and language, allowing thoughts just to be empty thoughts. They are not important.

If you are waiting at the bus stop for bus number 3, then the cars, the bikes, the bus number 4, the bus number 10 and so on are all irrelevant. I want bus number 3. Other buses stop, their door opens, they have nice comfortable seats inside and it's very tempting to get on but it is not bus number 3. It is like that in the meditation; many things are arising which could be important or necessary but they don't have the right number. In another situation we might well get on bus number 10, but in our meditation we are following the bus of the nose. That is all we do. We find the breath and we stay with the breath and whatever else is coming is irrelevant. We are like a child who wants to finish watching something on television when it's their bedtime.

—But how will I know what happens?

—You will never know what happens.

—But that's not possible – I have to know what happens.

—It is your bedtime. You have to let go.

—But I am in the middle of it!

—You still have to let go.

This is the real power of meditation. As the Buddha said, *'If you are waiting for the movie to be finished this samsara movie can run for a very long time!'* You would never get to bed. No wonder we are so tired!

What it involves is seeing that the real power is the power to name, and especially the power to rename. *'This is important.'* *'No it's not – because it is your bedtime.'* When it is your bedtime this TV programme is no longer important. Before your bedtime it *was* very important. That is to say, the value of the movie is not intrinsic to the movie; it is contextual and situational. So now that it's bedtime you turn the movie off. In the meditation we turn the thought off, not by stopping thinking, but by reframing the thought as irrelevant.

You may decide to stop smoking but there are still cigarettes. When you sit in a cafe and someone is having a coffee and a cigarette it floats through the air into your nose. When you were a smoker this would remind you that now is the time to have a cigarette, because coffee and cigarettes are such a perfect marriage. That person is still smoking, but I don't smoke, and you use the smell of the smoke to remind you that you don't smoke. The meaning that once seemed embedded inside the smell of the cigarette is reframed and now it is a reminder that I don't smoke. For as long as the object has the power we are at the mercy of our habits and assumptions.

What in the christian tradition is called God, in the buddhist tradition is called the mind. It is our mind that says whether something is good or bad. This world is created by the choices we make. Some people decide to become thieves; some people decide to go to clubs and have someone stick a fist up their arse. They are not dragged there by the police, no-one makes them go, they choose to go and have this experience. People can choose to have all kinds of experiences and they do this because it starts to become important for them. Looking at it from the outside, you might wonder why on earth anyone would you do that, but for the person who is in that experience it seems completely important.

This is the meaning of attachment in buddhism. On an outer level it means having a possession like a watch where a subject has ownership or possession of a particular object, but a more subtle form of attachment is merging, is when we become the object. We become the smoker, the alcoholic, the workaholic, or the worrier. We give ourself into that particular formation and that then becomes who we are.

The fresh open field of possibility is disregarded and abandoned by us because we give ourselves to our own fixations. Thus is why in the meditation we relax into the space. The space is very tolerant; it allows everything to be there without prejudice. The space is not telling what arises what it is. It is not saying this is good or this is bad. Once we attach valency or charge on to the arising object it becomes something or other, big or small, near or far, and so we don't see that it is just something arising and passing.

Of course, when you stop meditating and you get up and are out getting on with your life you have to make decisions. It's important that the kids get to school on time or that you pay you taxes on time and so on. In order to ensure that these things happen you make other things less important. Selection and making choices is part of our being in the world, but if we only do that we start to feel that many things are overly important. Our identification invests them with a deep significance which we then feel to be inherent in the object.

This is an illusion because if cigarettes were truly wonderful everyone would be smoking them. If a glass of wine for breakfast was a good idea then everybody would be drinking. The fact that some people start the day with an alcoholic drink doesn't mean it's a good idea in itself, but for some people that is what they do. *'If I don't have a drink, I don't feel so good.'* That is a relationship. It is not the truth of the object. This is difficult because what it means is that I am involved in everything; not one thing happens without my mental foundation. Either I do it automatically or I do it with awareness but one way or another I am always making judgments... about how people walk in the street, about the state of the trees... about litter on the pavement .. etc., I am always evaluating what is going on. From the buddhist point of view this is not something wrong, but it is something which has no inherent or intrinsic truth to it.

We know from christian and muslim history that the different sects used to fight each other. Different kinds of communists fight each other, but they are all communists and they are all christians, so why do they do that? Because it is the detail that is important. The detail is what I make to be important and this is how conflict arises. Instead of saying, *'This is what I choose and you are welcome to make your own choice because either way it is only a choice'*, we think, *'I have chosen this because it is true. I know that it's true because I am intelligent. You have not chosen it and this is a sign that you are not intelligent and first I will try to educate you by showing you the faults of your position and the virtues of mine. If necessary I will drop a bomb on you or shoot you. Make your choice. Agree with me or die.'*

YOU MAKE THE OBJECT SHINE BUT YOU THINK IT'S THE OBJECT DOING IT

In the old days theatres used to have limelight. Along the front of the stage they would have blocks of limestone and underneath a gas flame would heat up the lime and it would give out light. There was so much light from this wonderful lime, but if you turned off the gas flame it was dark again. We think the object is shining. Where is the gas supply?

Your own mind. You are making the object shine but you think it's the object that is shining.

Some people like motorcars and if they see a Ferrari they have to stop and look at it. I am not very interested in cars, so for me it is nothing. *'But James, you have to have a look!'* If I look I don't see what they see because they are looking with the eyes of love and I just see something on the road. This is the light of the heart that is making the object shine. Our faith, our life energy, goes into the object. In the funeral services that I have been to, the minister often says, *'The Lord giveth and the Lord taketh away. Blessed is the name of the Lord.'* when the body is being laid in the ground.

For us buddhists this is the mind. The mind gives life and the mind takes it back. *'I love you.' 'I don't love you anymore.'* Most of us have experienced this story in our life. What happened? This person who was so shining was shining with you; you were polishing them. Your friend might have said, *'Hey, I don't know what you see in him.'* "Oh, you just don't understand. He is so wonderful." It is in these simple moments that you can see that this is the mind. When you give yourself to the object, the object is shining. When this is not happening the gas is turned off and the object is now something very ordinary.

When we come to the meditation we are sitting in the centre of the gas supply company – On and Off. Every time you switch it on you recognise this you can switch it off again.

THREE 'A' GURU YOGA PRACTICE

Whenever you feel you are getting caught up in what is happening you just relax into the out breath and allow whatever is there to go.

The Three 'A' guru yoga practice is a simple support to help us enter into the state of relaxation. In the space in front of us we imagine a white letter 'A' about two arms' length in front of us. You can imagine it as a capital 'A' or if you know the Tibetan form you can use that. In the Sanskrit and Tibetan alphabets 'A' is the basic vowel which exists with all consonants. 'A' is the fundamental sound of the universe. It is the sound that children make and it becomes mama or papa and so on. 'A' represents emptiness, and emptiness is the potential for everything to occur. As we have looked several times, it is the emptiness of the mirror that allows it to show all the many different reflections. Emptiness doesn't mean 'nothing at all'; it is the space of hospitality within which things can manifest.

When we make the sound of 'A' all the thought constructions and the many diverse objects of the world can relax back into their ground nature of emptiness.

Around this letter 'A' we have the light of these five Tibetan traditional colours: white, red, blue, yellow and green. These colours represent the five elements and the five wisdoms and various buddhist understandings of how the world is manifesting. Out of emptiness potentiality arises in the diverse forms that we experience, but like a wave arising in the ocean, as the wave starts to manifest we see a wave but that wave has no individual identity. It is how the ocean shows itself. In the same way all the rich varieties of experiences are the formations of our own mind, not of our ego or our limited sense of self, but of the infinite open mind which is our ground.

We rest our gaze on this white letter 'A' with these rays of light around it and together we make the sound of Aa three times. This white 'A' is the mind and presence of the Buddha and of all the teachers. As we say Aa we open ourself into this – naked and unprotected – we are just with this. Sound comes out, and at the end of the third 'A' the white 'A' vanishes with the rainbow colours vanishing in space.

We just sit in space as we have done before and whatever comes, comes as different kinds of thoughts, feelings, sensations and sounds. We don't have to organise or control these or rearrange them; just let them be as they are and see what happens. The impulse to be involved, which is the impulse to identify with the subjective matrix, just let it arise and pass. If you invest it with your energy and you feel you have to think about this then the potential of the mind merges into your private individual subjectivity. That way you can spend the whole meditation time having one thought after another. Without merging, without separating, we just stay with it.

We are used to the idea of 'freedom from' and 'freedom to.' In the Tibetan language the word for Buddha is *sangye*, *sang* means pure and *gye* means spreading or increasing. *Sang* indicates free from all limitations: the pure state of wisdom. *Gye* means free to do whatever is necessary: the pure state of compassion. But there is another kind of freedom which is 'freedom with'. So, in the meditation when the thoughts, feelings and sensations arise, we are resting on the fine point between withdrawing and merging.

Using the example of the mirror, we have looked several times at how the reflection is in the mirror, but it doesn't contaminate the mirror. In the same way without merging into what is arising or identifying with it we are just present – very close – and through this we see that the openness of the mind is present with whatever is arising. It has the freedom to be with whatever is arising without getting lost. This is the union of wisdom and compassion. It is not about separation, but about trusting the indestructible nature of this spacious mind itself.

Three 'A' practice

We sit in a comfortable way with our skeleton carrying our weight. The gaze is open and resting in space. We are not staring at a distant wall. We have a sense of the white letter 'A'. For some people that kind of visualising or imagining is very easy and for others of us it is more difficult. The most important thing is just the feeling tone of openness and trust. We make the sound of 'A' three times together and sit in the practice.

This is a practice you can do several times a day. You can begin with just relaxing in the out breath. You can do it at work even if you only have two or three minutes. It opens up a space within which everything can be integrated and so is very helpful.

Of course sometimes you may want to add the Refuge and Bodhicitta prayers beforehand, but this is the actual practice of refuge. When you open and relax into the nature of the mind there is no higher refuge than this. When we meditate with our eyes open in this non-dual field of experience all beings are automatically included. Just by opening to your own nature Refuge and Bodhicitta are automatically available.

Verse 14: The nature of mind

What is called 'mind' cannot be identified as this or that. It is not an entity and it has no defining characteristics. If you search for it, it cannot be found for it has been empty from the very beginning without substantial essence. Empty, it is beyond expression, untouched by birth, death, coming and going. It is not created by any cause nor destroyed by any condition. It remains untouched in emptiness, free of increase or decrease, development and decline, or any kind of change.

'What is called the mind cannot be identified as this or that.' Whenever we come to some conclusion and we think, *'This is who I am and this is what my mind is'*, if we stay with it we find it was just another thought.

'It is not an entity and it has no defining characteristics.' An 'entity' generally is taken to means a thing which exists in itself. However when we consider any seemingly discrete entity we find that in fact its existence is relative for it 'exists' in relation to other things. Moreover the mind is not a thing. It cannot be found existing anywhere and the characteristics attributed to it are merely labels. Neither the mind nor what arises for the mind is an entity.

In the tradition they says it is like the sky. When we look at the sky we can see things. We see clouds, birds, and planes but we don't really see the sky as the gaze just goes straight through. The sky itself is unobstructive and this is its basis for hospitality. There is no quality that will give you a handle on the mind; whatever you say about it, is what you say about it.

This is what we were looking at first thing this morning. We can tell the world what it is and that creates a particular kind of knowledge, but we can also let the world show us what it is. You go out into the forest, you see a tree, and you say, *'Oh, this is an oak tree* and this is an acorn. The local pigs like to eat these acorns.' This will generate a particular relationship with the tree. But if you relax and just look at the tree, breathe it in, and let it come in through your eyes, you can't say anything, it's incredible. And then back you go to telling the tree what it is...

Nuden Dorje is saying here that there are no defining characteristics to the mind, and that we should be careful because we are very good at inventing defining characteristics. There is a saying that 'nature abhors a vacuum'. In the same way our ego consciousness likes to fill space with our own ideas until you end up with more and more of yourself. When you sit in the practice, if you find yourself naming and labelling what seems to be going on, you don't have to stop doing this; just open and be aware that this is the imagination and construction at work.

Our big problem is that we confuse construction with description. *'This is a beautiful tree. It is so old and strong and the shape is incredible.'* In that moment we think we are describing the tree but actually we are creating our tree. The bird that has its nest in the tree doesn't stop in mid-flight and think how beautiful its home is today; it is just flying into its nest. The tree is beautiful for us because we have the concepts and the cultural background and these factors come together to generate the idea that the tree is beautiful. For a logger the tree is money.

These interpretations are the activity of your mind. You think you are describing what is there but in fact you are creating what is there. Recognising that we have this capacity, we have to watch out when we are exploring the nature of our own mind so that we don't fill the space with our own thoughts and interpretations.

He continues: **'If you search for it, it cannot be found, for it has been empty from the very beginning without substantial essence.'** We have a mind but we cannot find it as something, but it seems to find us, because wherever we are our mind is here. So maybe we don't have to find it since it is already here. If it weren't here, we wouldn't be here. Where is the mind? Where we are. Not 'here' like something sitting on our shoulder; not 'here' like some essence hidden inside us; but 'here' beyond thought and imagination and not like anything else.

'Empty, it is beyond expression, untouched by birth, death, coming and going.' Our thoughts have a beginning and an end. Our jobs, our shopping, our cleaning, our housekeeping have a beginning and an end. All the aspects of our daily life have a beginning, a middle and an end. The stories we tell about our lives have a beginning, a middle and an end, but our mind doesn't since it has never been born. That is to say, it has never come into existence as some-*thing* and not having been born how can it die?

Consciousness is born and dies. We are conscious of the weather. After some months it will be much hotter. In the middle of the summer you cannot have the consciousness of this weather now. The way in which we apprehend this particular moment in time is unique and specific to the organising factors of beginning, middle, and end meeting together. We seem to be able to get a grasp on what is happening because 'beginning, middle, and end' means that something is finite: beginning means that something was, before now is here, and end means that what was here is now not here.

Everything that has a shape can be grasped in some way, which brings us back to logos. By naming you apprehend, but you cannot apprehend the mind. The mind is a quality of being, however 'being' is a difficult term because we are used to thinking that something is this or that. With the verb 'to be' we say this is an apple, and if it is an apple then it is not a pear or a banana. So in this sense, being is something specific.

THE MIRROR NEVER GETS TIRED OUT

When we say the mind is like 'being' we mean that it is a presence: it is here but not *as* something. Strange. Not like anything else... Mmm... That means that all the knowledge and skills and experience that I have developed by taking hold of the world are irrelevant in relation to the mind. If I apply them in relation to the mind I will create my own fantasy of my mind, but this will not be the mind itself. The mind gives itself; hence it is the ground of being.

'It is not created by any cause nor destroyed by any conditions.' This is the unchanging nature of the mind: it is *vajra* or *dorje* meaning indestructible. Reflections do not destroy the mirror or impact it in any way.

When you drove here you travelled many kilometres burning up gasoline in the petrol tank and making some wear on the tyres. You have side mirrors on the car showing many images along the way. After a while you check the tyres, maybe you add some oil, you'll need to fill up with gasoline, but you don't look at the car mirrors to check if they are exhausted. You don't think, *'I will take the mirrors to the Mirror Hotel for a little rest before our journey home.'* The mirror is always working but it never gets tired. This is an example of the mind: the image doesn't tire the mirror, thoughts don't tire the mind.

All the experiences we have had in our life: happiness, sorrow, anxiety, loneliness and so on, create some kind of wear and tear with our sense of self, but the mind itself doesn't get tired.

Whether we understand this or not is a kind of litmus test: if we are getting caught up in these constructions it is a sign that we are established in our ego sense. All we have to do is relax; the one thing we don't have to do is try harder. You can't try hard to go to sleep; you let yourself fall into sleep. You let yourself relax and open. You find your way of being, and this involves trust and relaxation.

'It remains untouched in emptiness free of increase and decrease, development and decline, or any kind of change.' Whatever physicists say, space doesn't expand or contract. Things expand and contract but in dzogchen space is like the womb of the Great Mother; it is the arena in which manifestation or movement is occurring. It is always the same, always with one taste – the taste of emptiness – and everything in it has the taste of emptiness. The rich diversity of movement, of experience, and of all possibilities of life are inseparable from the space. This doesn't develop or get better and neither does it decline.

We know that if we sit trying to do some meditation some days it seems easy and other days more difficult. It might be good for some weeks and then it suddenly seems impossible: you sit down but you are just distracted. How is this possible? Marching onward ever upwards. No, it is not like that. These are thoughts and sometimes thoughts are clear and sometimes they are not clear. With a lot of effort you can develop your thoughts. Perhaps when you were at school you learned another language and had your accent, your grammar, and vocabulary corrected. You developed your capacity to speak that language. What Nuden Dorje is saying here is that the mind is not like that: it is not cumulative, or developed on the basis of memory, because it is not an entity or a thing.

The mind is complete and perfect from the very beginning, it has never been developed, and this is why it is called *dzogpa chenpo*, the great completion. It just is, without beginning or end, top or bottom. Its very absence of defining qualities allows it to give birth to the whole of samsara and nirvana.

ONE GROUND: TWO PATHS

Generally in dzogchen they say there is one ground and two paths. The one ground is the mind itself. One path is to see how the mind is; then the mind shows itself as being the *dharmadhatu*. *Dhatu* means realm or space within which all dharmas or phenomena occur. What we have been looking at is that dharmas are not things.

A tree doesn't exist by itself. Clearly the tree has roots in the earth that depend on the amount of minerals in the earth and the amount of rain it gets and that is its relative interdependence. But what we call a tree is what we call a tree. The dharma, or the phenomenon, or the thing which we imagine being out there by itself, comes into existence through our apprehension. This is vital for our understanding. There are no separate existing entities; mind is with everything. What we take to be things are actually experiences.

The object that we experience is subject to change. In the course of the day the sun moves across the sky so the light coming in the window shifts and illuminates the room in different ways. We can say we are in the same room but this is an idea, an abstraction, or a concept. The actuality of being here in a living breathing body is that the room shows itself depending on the movement of the light. There is no room. There is a flow of experience which we organise with our concept *of 'This is a room, and it is the same room that we have been in for several days.'* 'Same' means that there is sufficient seeming continuity to allow me to apply the title 'same' to the room. The pillars haven't moved because if they moved the ceiling would fall down. We say, *'Thank you for being reliable pillars.'*

This is where it gets very strange. I look at the pillar and what do I see? I see shape and colour and the colour is changing according to the way the light is coming through the window. The pillar is changing! Oh no, the roof will fall in! The pillar is the same. This is it – life and death. The life is the changing nature of the room. *'You have got to be here and see how it is all changing!'* "Nah.. It's the same old room with nothing new to look at." So you can take it for granted and fall asleep in your assumptions, but what is here? It is fresh.

This is the issue. The raw revealing quality of our world is always fresh and changing. Once you live, not in the actual world of the senses as they reveal themselves, but in the realm of thought, then you get solidification; there seem to be things with their own essence and substance. When we read a term like *dharmadhatu* it refers to the space of the potential of the flow of experience. *Dharmadhatu* is not referring to a kind of storage space packed full of a lot of stuff, but to the ceaseless flow of the revelation of experience.

Verse 15: The Ground of Everything

'Free of the four limiting notions of existence, non-existence, both existence and non-existence, neither existence nor non-existence, and of all relative positions mind is emptiness, uncompounded. Free of artifice from the very beginning, awareness remains unimpeded. When this is experienced youthful, fresh awareness is released from its covering pot and you see your own face, the natural mode of infinite goodness (Samantabhadra).'

'Free of the four limiting notions of existence, non-existence, both existence and non-existence, neither existence nor non-existence, and of all relative positions mind is emptiness, uncompounded' These four positions are very common in buddhist philosophy and Nagarjuna in particular is famous for the way he shows that each has the nature of emptiness. Concepts are very seductive, or rather, consciousness makes use of concepts in order to create a kind of clarity, but they are an illusion.

We could say, as an example, that this building exists – it is here and it seems to just exist – but it exists on the basis of the earth being underneath. If there was an earthquake it wouldn't exist. Or if people stopped coming to Aracena then this hotel would become bankrupt and it might be knocked down. The existence of the building is relative to many other factors which are outside the building. When we say that the building exists we have the sense it exists in itself, but its seemingly permanent existence is dependent on people coming in and out of the front door. The building exists in relation to people coming to stay in the hotel; it doesn't exist in itself.

The fact that it has a dependent existence doesn't mean that it doesn't exist at all, because something is here, but what is here is because of factors which are not here: for example, the architect's imagination to make a building like this. It is a little bit old fashioned in its style. If someone were building a new hotel today it probably wouldn't be exactly like this. The existence of the building now is dependent on the time that the architect went to college and got his diploma and the contract, and his mother was very pleased. *'My son created this.'* All of that is part of the building: the causal factors in the past, the maintenance factors in the present, and the factors of destruction in the future are all part of the existing of the building, and therefore it neither exists nor doesn't exist. Being free of all relative positions means whatever you say about the building can only ever be partially true; you can't catch the actual building.

We are sitting here together now in what we might call the same room. Most of you are looking at me and the translator and Juan and I are looking at you. We see something different from you. This is what we see and this is our experience. This is the room for us but you get another room, so to say it is the same room is an idea. The millions of rooms which exist in this room is the actuality of the room. The room is a potential which is awakened by the way that you are present here: your own history, whether you are interested in art or design, whether you find the seat uncomfortable; all of these factors influence the room for you.

There is no objective room and there is no right way to experience the room. The room is a site of generosity offering itself for interpretation which means you are a co-creator of the room. The world depends on you. You are not the master. You are not the slave. You are the co-creator of everything you encounter. Because you can create shit there is no need to be stupid. You just have to come to London to see all the ugly inappropriate buildings that architects are creating; it is mind boggling and insane. We are co-creators but even if we are not architects or painters or decorators we create with our interpretations.

This is a very unusual way of looking at things. Usually we think something is there. We start with the noun and then we add the interpretation, using adverbs and adjectives etc. A beautiful room, an ugly room, a small room etc, but the room is there. From the point of view of this text, this is not the case; the room comes into being through your participation. The room is evoked. This doesn't mean it is sleeping. It is not like Sleeping Beauty deep in the forest covered with brambles and you come along and cut your way through like some brave hero and awaken her with a kiss. There is no Sleeping Beauty to be found precisely because as soon as you come near her, she wakes up. The world comes to meet us as we go to the world.

This is what is meant by co-emergence. It is not subject onto object, or object onto subject' it is this ceaseless flow of emergence, of arising with our participation. We are not the magus, the great magician, calling things into being. The world arises with us as a togetherness – a collaboration – and Nuden Dorje is saying that whenever you take up a definite position of *'it's like this'* or *'it's like that'* this is mental structure. It is not how it is because the mind is empty.

Seeing this, it is important not to get confused since it is quite a simple idea. It means ungraspable – empty of anything that would give you a hold. You don't have to take it because you already have it. The world gives itself to you moment by moment – here it is. The girl wants to be kissed and the world is ready. This is very important.

Emptiness means availability. Not sealed off inside something-ness, but the generosity of our potential which is always available and, importantly, a potential which cannot be known in advance. Since we don't know what's going to happen, don't fall asleep in your assumptions. If you are here, spot on, each moment will always be fresh, but if you approach it through knowing in advance you will be grasping at shadows and there is no satisfaction in that. This is the emptiness of the mind – it is not a thing.

'Free of artifice from the very beginning awareness remains unimpeded.' Artifice here means 'being created', becoming something in particular. Because there is nothing fixed, every view of whatever it is, is valid.

Aracena seems to be a nice town, but it is quite a small town. Last night was Saturday and Maria went out to meet her José. When she went around the corner she saw José with someone else. They were standing very close to one another and José had his hand on her bum. Maria was watching, *'You bastard! My hopes are dashed! I hate this whole town!'* Such things happen in life. Suddenly the whole town is reborn in her mind as some shit place because now Maria is thinking that maybe everyone else already knew that José had another girl and she was the last one to know. *'You're supposed to be my friend. Did you know that José was doing this? Why did you not tell me? Now I don't trust anyone.'*

We create worlds and suddenly they are destroyed. Whatever is created will be destroyed. Couples stay together for a long time but still one of them will die before the other. Artificiality comes from building up images and pictures, but the mind is not like that. From the very beginning it has never been created as a structure and therefore it is unimpeded.

José is indefinable; he is my 'gorgeous bastard.' Any opinion about José can be applied to José because he will appear in different ways according to different circumstances. Gossip is very nice. *'Hey, you know what José is like, he's always up to tricks.'* But of course we never know José; there is always more to José than anybody knows, including his mother. This is very important because when we grasp things we totalise them, we seem to have the whole of them, but what you get is always a part and there is always more.

'Unimpeded' here means that anything can be anything. The beautiful car which is the owner's pride and joy can be the cause of a child's death. These are readings or interpretations.

'When you come into the direct presence that the mind is like this, youthful fresh awareness is released from its covering pot and you see your own face, the natural mode of infinite goodness.' If you have a lamp or a small candle and you put a big pot over it no light comes out. The light is there, it hasn't been put out, but it is covered. So what is covering the light of the mind?

Moment by moment new experiences are arising and we are here, but being here we drift off and our attention wanders with some thought of the past or the future. This is the pot, the light of the mind, the natural clarity which is the showing of everything, and which is not available when we are caught up in thoughts. We only have the thoughts because of the clarity of the mind which shows the thoughts, so the display or the radiance of the illuminating clarity of the mind is itself the obscuration. Without the radiance of the mind you are not aware of any thoughts or feelings or sensations, but due to fixation on the thought as the central form, the ground or the basis or the illuminating power is taken for granted and forgotten.

When I was a child, particularly at the weekends when we had more time to eat peacefully together, my father would say, *'Now, thank your mother for cooking the food.'* I remember being quite amazed as mothers do the cooking, that's just what they do. Bicycles go on the road...footballs get kicked around... and mums do cooking...so what are you going to thank? You don't thank the football, so why do you thank your mother? The function of the mother is to be invisible. She should do everything and not get in the way. My father thought that to have children like me was terrible!

We are like this with the mind. The mind is our mother providing everything moment by moment without getting tired or complaining.

How do we reward her? We take her for granted and pretend she doesn't exist. This is the meaning of ignorance: the food is just on the table; the dishes just wash themselves.

—*I am going out to play*

—*No, you help your mother. Your mother sits here with me and we have a coffee and you boys do the dishes.*

—*But why do we have to?*

It's a big resistance – things don't happen by themselves.

This is what is meant, so that when we start to take these assumptions off, which are themselves ideas arising from the mind, then we see your own face. Our own face is the natural radiance of the mind shining out as everything which is arising. Not the face of the ego – your historically developed profile – but the face that has been there from the very beginning. Our face is how we show, and when we meet people we look at their face and ask how they are. 'Our original face' means the mind showing itself just as it is.

Verse 16: The Beginning of Samsara

'If that is not realised awareness loses continuity and becomes stupid. This is called 'co-emergent ignorance'. Appearances and emptiness are falsely split and are experienced as separate things. Bound by the fetter of grasping subject and graspable object the ignorance of reificatory identification develops.'

'If you are not awake to the fact of that inseparability of the ground and the manifestation then awareness loses continuity and becomes stupid.' He starts to show what happens when this is not recognised.

It means that awareness merges into consciousness, meaning attention to particulars. You start to get caught up in stuff. If you walk uphill to the castle you can look out and see the hills and trees and everything is there, but when you come down from the castle into the streets you see much less. Everything is still there but you have entered into a place that has less openness. Nothing has changed. The trees and the hills haven't vanished but now you see the street and the parked cars. It is not that you go from one land to another land. You don't fall out of happiness into this horrible place somewhere else, but you find yourself situated in a positioning which reveals a more narrow vista.

He says this is called 'co-emergent ignorance'. Co-emergent means that the openness and the closure are there together.

I know that Aracena is surrounded by hills, but standing here in this street I can't see any hills. The hills are there but they are not there for me. You could say I am in a street or in a town with many hills, but the more I give my attention to the detail of the houses, to the way the stones are used to pave the road... the more the details pull me into the particulars. The idea that there are hills and valleys becomes some abstract concept. I have even lost the context of the street by being over immersed in the street. The hills are there but I am ignoring them by attending to what is here, and the more I attend to what is here the more the presence of the hills vanishes for me.

Somebody suggests going for a walk, but you are down on your knees with a small toothbrush trying to polish the paving stones and thinking, *'This is my street. I cannot go out until all the stones are clean.'* Fifty years later, when you are dead, they may be able to place the coffin on very clean stones! At that point, they take you out of the street into the hills!

So, Nuden Dorje is pointing out to us that our attention gets pulled into thoughts, feelings and sensations and the more we go into this detail, the more we have our own private world built up with an accumulation of 'things-that-happened-to-me'. We start to attribute value to the things in the world according to their significance for us.

'Appearances and emptiness are falsely split and are experienced as separate things.' This is the central point. Awareness is the panoramic vision. I am sitting here at the moment with my gaze open, in a panoramic style, and in the middle I can see a green pillar. If I focus my attention on the green pillar the panoramic vision narrows. That is what he is meaning here. Everything is still here but appearance, the particular, the specific, captures my attention as I start to name it. In order to get a precise definition I have to bring in other ideas. I think, *'The colour of the pillar is a kind of lime green, but there is some kind of darker shading there as well. That bit reminds me of this painting by Monet...'* My whole world is now being put onto the pillar and it seems to become more and more important, so that now I only have pillar-ness. The pillar is being extrapolated from its ground, its world. This is what we do with naming and applying our knowledge and associations.

Everything appearing together, unfolding, showing its empty potential in which appearance was the rich appearance of emptiness as a ceaseless flow of fresh moments. It now seems to have the sense of appearing as discrete separate things that can be identified more precisely. For example, in this room there are men and women, some are younger, some are older, some are taller, some are shorter; we can apply various criteria for sorting out different groups of people. This allows us to make groupings of people. On the basis of seeing someone as a member of a group we can now make a prediction about individuals since *'they are in that family because they share qualities'*.

Although I have never seen this kind of potato before I don't need to go through some elaborate 'getting to know you' experience because a potato is a potato. You can roast, fry, mash or boil potatoes. But we do have particular kinds of potatoes, so is it a new potato with very flaky skin? If it is a new potato I put it under the tap and rub the skin off and then I boil it served with butter and maybe a little mint on top, You wouldn't roast or fry it as this would be abuse of a baby new potato. Boiling is bad enough, but don't cut it up before it's dead! In life you learn about potatoes and about different kinds of onions too. In Spain you have so many kinds of tomatoes. You are the boss of the tomato, but the tomato also has a voice. The tomato looks at you with your knife and says, *'You want to put me in a salad? Are you stupid?! I belong in soup.'*

In that way we come into this dialogue with the world. The more ideas, concepts and memories that we have, the more we can go into the fine details of the forms that we find. The richness of the world is now a multitude of things and so emptiness vanishes. Each thing seems solid, real, and important in itself. We are now in the job of managing the potential of the world in order to create the best outcome for ourselves where 'ourself' is also an historically developed patterning.

'Bound by the fetter of grasping subject and grasping object, the ignorance of reificatory identification develops.' The more we take hold of the seeming objects in the world, the more separate and solid they appear, and our response to them becomes more particular.

To continue with cooking... Cooking is very interesting for exploring this, especially mushrooms. First of all you have to know if the mushrooms are going to poison you or not. Many edible mushrooms require specific ways of cooking. Some can be lightly fried in butter whereas others need soaking to take out some strains of poison. *'Oh, no, don't do that! This kind of mushroom needs this. Doing this is really important because if you do that you will spoil it.'* This is how we talk: it is getting smaller and smaller. This is also our human culture, that we shouldn't spoil the food.

However here we are working with the potential of the mushroom, allowing the mushroom to show itself rather than dominating or controlling it. We work collaboratively with the mushroom.

When I was about eleven years old, my father became a bit ill and my brother and I went to stay with my aunt. I remember very clearly that my aunt made scrambled eggs but she made them in a way that my mother never did. I looked at this thing on my plate and I missed my mummy because my eggs weren't right. What is this? My aunt asked if I wanted scrambled eggs. I said *'Yes'* because I like scrambled eggs, but I don't get scrambled eggs; I get something else. And she thought this was scrambled eggs!

Most children have an experience like this. We have a little category and we know what something is and then we realise that this is just in my family, and other people do it in another way. This could open us up or we might think we never want to do that again,

When I am not in England, I never drink tea. I may ask for a cup of tea and what do I get? A cup of warm water with a tea bag on the side! How cold does the water have to be before you put the tea bag in? Spain has signed up to the international convention for the protection of tea bags. I don't understand this because you are quite happy to boil a live lobster but you won't put the tea bag in the boiling water! I know what tea is and it's not that. This is what it means. Dharma is not about some other realm; it is exactly about our daily life.

With this increasing level of involvement comes the second level of ignorance, which he calls **'reificatory identification'**. It means that I am the one doing the identifying. I am telling the world what it is and this allows me to seem able to control what is out there. Simultaneously, it gives me the confidence of feeling I know what is going on, and so my relationship with the world is mediated through language, concepts, and the accumulation of ideas. The sparkling freshness of the moment is obscured by my own intelligence because 'I know what something is'.

When members of a Middle Eastern extremist group are filmed cutting off a prisoner's head, they seem to do it without fear or shame because they 'know they are right'. They know who they are killing. They are killing someone who should be killed. And so you should kill them. They even appear quite proud of what they have done. This is a kind of knowledge: *'I know who you are. You are the sort of person who shouldn't be on this earth so killing you is good.'* There is a logic to this and people clearly feel confident and clear that what they are doing is right. The conflicts that we have all over the world arise because people see the world 'as it is' and therefore, *'What I say is true because this is how it is. If you don't agree with me then clearly you are wrong'*. This is how conflicts arise. This is a strange paradox because the more knowledgeable I become, the more ignorant I become since I am ignoring what is there.

An example of this is the water supply to Aracena. The engineers say they can build a dam in the hills and get a good supply of water for the city. They set out their plans which are completely logical and a good idea. But then along comes the ecologist who says that in this valley there is a beetle with big horns, and here is the only place in Spain where these beetles exist. The ecologist produces a document of over five hundred pages that includes the mating practices of the big-horned beetle, so to build a dam like this is a crime against the beetle. Both sets of people are intelligent, having gone to university and done a lot of training, but they are looking at the situation with completely different sets of assumptions.

What seems real and true inside one frame of reference looks wrong to the other position: *'I don't understand, why can't you see what is right in front of you? It is so obvious.'* But it is only obvious inside this one blinkered frame of reference and this, of course, is one of the tragedies of our human situation. People can have a very good intention and be very intelligent and work very hard, but it just creates chaos because each of us is just seeing one little slice of the cake.

It is as if you were walking over the hills and as you go up and down the contour at each moment you stop and look around and what you see is there, but it's the view from *here*. You take ten steps more, you look again, and it's a different view, step by step by step, but we are always located somewhere. We speak the truth of the view *from here*, which is true for here, but 'here' is not the whole world. This is the real difficulty. How come we make so many problems when we become more and more intelligent?

Verse 17: 'I' and 'me'

'Non-existent and existent things are both grasped at as real. Being bound by the confusion of self-identification you experience a self doing the grasping. With notions of 'I' and 'me' developing in your stream of consciousness as the cause of developing attraction and aversion, there arises the samsaric activity of the afflictions of the five poisons of stupidity, aversion, attraction, pride and jealousy. From one cause many other causes arise (that is to say, all the complexity of samsara).'

'Non-existent and existent things are both grasped at as real.' An example of an existent thing is us being in this room just now, as there seems to be something here. A non-existent thing can refer to the future as it doesn't exist nor do we know how it is going to be even though we make all sorts of plans for future eventualities. Maybe that future will never arise but anyway I feel able to have some certainty about future possibilities since I have pulled these factors into my frame of reference and that gives me the sense of being in control.

'Being bound by the confusion of self-identification you experience a self doing the grasping.'

I might have some sensation in my stomach and then say, 'I feel hungry'; or I could say that feelings of hunger are emerging. Who are they emerging for? Me. I then join these two together and say, *'I am hungry.'* By taking a sensation to be a truth about me I mobilise myself as an agent: as the one who makes things happen.

I can tell what time it is. I pick up the watch and I look at it and I see that fifteen minutes have gone. I am 'telling the time'. I am actually interpreting the movements of the hands on the dial of my watch, and when I was small I didn't know how to do that. I learned, or I internalised patterns of identification which we describe as 'being able to tell the time'. I lift the watch in front of me and I look at it, and there arises in my mind *'Oh, it's twenty five past one.'* This thought came to me. I am saying it's twenty-five past one because somebody told me it's twenty-five past one. Who told me? I told me. But I didn't tell me – the thought came in my mind and this thought came on the basis of having my mother kindly explain again and again how the watch works. Having built up that habit – the outer form – the watch – triggers the arising of the internal formation which gives rise to the sense that it's twenty-five past one.

And now flies the cuckoo who, as we know, doesn't like to make a nest for its own eggs. Here is a nice nest. Watch. Twenty-five past one. Quite comfortable. The cuckoo lays an egg and the egg opens. *'I can tell the time! I am here! Cuckoo! Cuckoo!'* 'I' is in inserted into this process. I am doing it. But the thought 'twenty-five past one' came to me. I didn't push it out from my 'James factory,' I found it and it's mine. *'I did it. I can tell the time.'* This is the automatisation of the flow of thoughts and the patterning is going on and on.

I imagine when you meet together and are talking that you don't have a thought in the back of your mind that you are speaking Spanish. You are just speaking. But if somebody asked, *'What language do you speak?'* *"I am speaking Spanish."* You step outside of this flow and it becomes something that you have, that you own, and that you do. The insertion of this empty signifier 'I' takes onto itself the mantle, the habit, the protection of being the one that is able to do.

'With notions of 'I' and 'me' developing in your stream of consciousness as the cause of developing attraction and aversion, there arises the samsaric activity of the five poisons of stupidity, aversion, attraction, pride and jealousy.'

We already looked at that in some detail on the first day here: something happens and there is a feeling of liking or not liking which gets refined as 'I like,' or 'I don't like,' which is then projected out as 'this is good' or 'this is bad'. If it is good I want it, and if it's bad I don't want it. We have attraction or desire, or aversion or anger, based on our notion of the object that we see as self-existing and out there having intrinsic qualities. This is how it feels for us. We look and we think no. For someone else however it's yes, but for us it's no because we don't like it. *'I don't like this, it doesn't taste good to me.'* In that way the world gets chopped up into more and more particular entities which each seem to have their own valency or quality.

Arising from this are the so-called five poisons or five afflictions. The first one, stupidity, is the mental dullness that comes from relying on our own assumptions; something has become a truth for us and on the basis of that things become foregrounded or pushed into the background. This mental darkness or fogginess is called *ti-muk (Tib. Ti-Muk)* in Tibetan. It means that the openness of the world and the freshness of everything is no longer available for us because we have prejudice. We don't think we are prejudiced; we think we are just speaking the truth of our lives.

For example, I have no interest in football; it doesn't mean anything for me. Football is very important for many people and they get a lot of joy out of it but that door is closed for me by *timuk*. I don't have access to it now so part of the world has gone dead for me. Think of all the many opportunities of culture and travel that we ignore and dismiss. So much of the world is put in the darkness. *'It's not for me. I don't like it. I went once with my grandmother when I was six and it was horrible. I will never do that again – once was enough.'* The world is being chopped up.

Stupidity is a very important idea as essentially it means bias: we approach the world already turned. There are many kinds of clothes we would never wear, books we would never read, food we would never eat, places we would never go, and movies we would never watch. We switch off the lights, but luckily some things still shine. *'I know what I like, and I like what I know.'* This is written on the t-shirt of the stupid. Why would I choose anything else when I know what I like? This is how the mind becomes narrow and small. A door opens a little, you sniff the wind, and close the door. Stupidity doesn't mean being unintelligent; it means dulling your sensibility so that so much of the world becomes closed to you and on the basis of that you have aversion, attraction, pride and jealousy

'From one cause many other causes arise.' From the one cause of ignoring the open ground of being, the spacious awareness which includes everything moment by moment and which is a generous hospitality open to everything, can end up as this one particular person with his or her likes and dislikes walking through the big forest on a very narrow path. This is called samsara.

The plans that we make for life can be changed very quickly. We are very vulnerable. We may become sick or unemployed and our whole idea of who we are gets changed. Perhaps we can no longer find anywhere to apply the particular skills we have developed. For example in the 1980's Britain started closing down her coal mines. Generally the coal miners lived all together in coal mining villages consisting and their jobs and skills were passed down in families. To be a coal miner was to be quite something! There is a kind of special bonding among people whose jobs take them into physical danger. Most of the villages had their own brass band and choirs and festivals. All this was in place, existed, and then the mines closed. All the things that miners knew about tunnelling under the ground and working together safely were skills that didn't fit anywhere else any more. These men were not wanted, were 'redundant', and became useless.

I experienced this in the 1970's when the shipyards on the River Clyde were being closed. All these engineers and steelworkers who were used to managing huge plates of steel, bending and riveting, were now nothing. They had nothing to get up for in the morning because their dignity was their work. They looked like ghosts of the men they had been. Previously they had been the family breadwinners and had put food on the table. All this made them feel like a somebody, a man and a father.

It was the same in the small fishing towns around Scotland. The EU's policy was to protect the fish stocks even if it meant killing the fishermen. The directive was that fishermen could only go fishing for forty days a year. What do you do now with a boat that you can only use for forty days a year? So people got another job and didn't want to go back to fishing. The raison d'être of the village collapses. The harbour nearest to me when I was a child had about forty or fifty small fishing boats, and now the boats are yachts and other pleasure boats owned by rich people from all over the world.

These are very sad stories for me because these were very good hard-working people whose lives were changed by causes and conditions operating somewhere else. They are all proof of what Nuden Dorje says here: that if you think you are living securely and permanently in whatever definition of yourself then be a little careful. Don't make your life narrow; don't over-invest in one small pattern. Keep your mind relaxed and open. Observe how the world is. Doing this will keep you light, flexible, and responsive.

Verse 18: Recognising the falsity

'When you understand the falsity of your confusion remain unartificially, effortlessly in the natural mode – the dharmakaya'

An example of what is meant here by the 'falsity of your confusion' is if you are driving in unknown countryside and turn on to a road that you think is the right way but after a while you are not so sure. However you decide you just have to keep on driving. Whereas if you recognise that you have taken the wrong road then you won't increase your suffering. Our falsity is our misapprehension: we thought that we recognised something clearly but we were wrong.

When you are driving along a road in the summertime you might see a mirage that looks like water; it is quite convincing, but it is not water. We are taken in by an illusion. The fact that it looks like water when there is no water is an illusion. If we believe the illusion to be true then that is what is called delusion. If you follow delusion you have confusion, because now you are fused with something which is not true but that you think is true.

'I need a cigarette.' This is a delusion and many people feel this. Really and truly they do not need a cigarette. Read the packet. It is even written there that smoking can kill you. *'But this is my favourite brand. I need this.'* It feels true, but it's not true. In various ways, with different things, whether it is with food or clothes or whatever, I am sure we all have had this kind of experience.

For example, I have many thousands of books at home. Given that I was dyslexic as a child this is a bit strange. I still read very slowly and usually I am also writing when I read. I read about six pages an hour so it is easy to see that 90% of the books I own I have not yet read. I clearly remember going into a second-hand bookshop in a small English town about six years ago. They had an illustrated one hundred year-old edition of a book I like very much, *'A Pilgrim's*

PROGRESS'. I already had four copies of this book. The book was exquisitely illustrated but since it cost £50 I didn't buy it. I still remember this book and every now and then I think I should go back as it might still be there. This is what the mind is like: I need yet another book that I will never read before I die.

When we observe our lives we see these things are true. We buy clothes we never wear because it seems important at the time. We put the meaning into the object and then it seems real: *'If I don't get this thing I will be unhappy.'* But it is only me who is making it important. This is our own falsity. This is how we cheat ourselves. We project meaning and value onto the object and then we imagine that meaning and value is inherent in the object and we become desperate to have the object. But the object is ourselves! We are caught by our own energy.

—*This is really important for me because I think it's important.*

—*Why do I think it's important?*

—*Because I have a habit of making unimportant things important. It is how I protect myself from boredom and despair.*

This is the mind. It is not that we are mad or stupid or bad but these are patterns of identification that we get caught up in.

Nuden Dorje tells us that once we see what we are doing then just relax and observe this and don't enter into judgement about it. Once we start thinking we are a bad or stupid person we only make life more difficult. It is just that life puts a little spin on things and we get caught in the spin. At the side of a river you sometimes see a little pool and a leaf has got caught there and is swirling around as the water in the pool gets turned by the flow of the river. The leaf is in the water and the water is not different from the water in the river, but the very movement of the river is turning the water in the side pool thereby keeping the leaf trapped. The point that Nuden Dorje is making here is that it is the very energy of the mind which is making a prison for us.

Right back to the earliest buddhist teachings the same point is made. In THE DHAMMAPADA, is a verse, 'Not *father, not mother, not sister, not brother, not friend, not enemy, nobody can help you like yourself,*' and then it repeats the same list of people and says nobody can *harm* you like yourself. The help we need is not out there. The harm we fear is not out there. What harms us is our own confusion and our capacity to cheat ourselves, to do something when we don't need to.

We are at the mercy of voices. What we call the ego is voices. Voices are ideas, thoughts, feelings and sensations which arise inside us and which seem to convey an important meaning. How will we know if they are right or wrong? We have to see them and we have to be with them. '*But I have given myself to this since I am sure it's true.*'

What is the difference between an impulse and spontaneity? An impulse is a pattern we have already developed; we prepared it earlier and put it in the freezer. A situation arrives...go to the freezer...to the microwave... to the plate... yum yum, very tasty! Spontaneity is fresh cooking. You are with the ingredients of a potential situation and you are cooking something new; it is quick but it is lively and fresh. An impulse is also quick but since you have done it before and you know what it will be like, it tastes a bit stale as. '*I need a cigarette.*' How many cigarettes have you had? Any benefit? No, not really. '*But I need a cigarette.*' The habit catches us; it looks new but it's old. We cheat ourselves. Nobody is forcing us to do these things.

THE SELF-LIBERATION OF CONFUSION

It is the same when we sit in meditation. We follow the thought which takes us again and again on little journeys here, there, and everywhere, ending up nowhere, yet we keep going after the thought. If you just allow the thought to go by, you are here. But if you get on to the thought you don't know where you are. Luckily another thought is coming along – I'll get on that one – maybe it will take me home. After a time you have been on so many buses you don't know where home is!

Yesterday we were talking about how the common word in Tibetan for sentient beings is *drowa*, which means someone who is travelling or going or moving. We never arrive anywhere and yet we have to keep on going otherwise how will I be here? But there is nothing here... *'Ah ha! Here comes a thought.'* When you relax into the space there is nothing here. *'Oh! Here's a bus coming along.'* This takes you off again.

So how do we relax into space without being annihilated? The presence of emptiness is neither existent nor non-existent, nor both existent and non-existent, nor neither existent nor non-existent; it is not anything.

When you are used to standing on solid ground you have a sensitivity to when the ground is unsurfaced. If you are walking on the hills and there are some loose rocks you can feel this. You want solid ground. But when you have a big slope of small rocks, called shale or screed, on the side of a hill, you can learn to run across it. You have to always move upwards with a regular fast-moving easy step as the hillside starts slipping, but because your angle is slightly up you can go across the shale. This is how we live in samsara. The ground is always dissolving underneath our feet so we keep moving and this movement keeps us keeping on. If you are off-balance but keep moving you won't fall over.

The ego is always off balance, but because we are moving we don't fall over which is why there is no end to samsara. Your own movement may stop you falling but it doesn't get you upright. You are trapped in this kind of limbo – not dead – not really relaxed and alive either – always moving – always something happening. This is what the text means by 'my falsity'. I imagine I know who I am and what I am doing with my life, but I am not grounded or centred or at home in my own skin which all keeps me very busy.

Nuden Dorje is not telling us to try harder or renounce what we are doing or become somebody else. He is telling us to remain effortlessly in the natural mode, which is the mind of all the buddhas.

Remember stillness and movement? The energy of the mind is always moving; the mind itself never moves. When you find yourself caught up in moving – in thoughts, feelings, memories and so on – notice that you have become merged in the energy of the mind. The energy of the mind is always inseparable from the mind itself, so without changing anything, relax into the mind which is the ground of the moving thoughts full, as they are, of confused ideation. This is the self-liberation of confusion.

One of the things that most children learn quite easily is the joy of spinning; it doesn't cost anything. You just spin round very fast and then you stop and you are off-balance and dizzy. This is the cheapest drug available. You, yourself, make yourself feel funny. If you stop spinning you will be quite grounded, but if you keep spinning you will get dizzy. That is all the Buddha ever said. Spinning is ignorance; just stand still. *'But it's boring to just stand still!'* Fair enough. Off you go then and enjoy your samsara!

THE WHOLE OF SAMSARA IS EVERYBODY PRETENDING TO BE LIKE EVERYBODY ELSE

Verse 18 is a short verse but it is a very important one because it is saying that you are not going from A to B. It is not saying that there is something wrong with you and that if you try harder you can become better. It is saying that your falsity is inseparable from the mind of all the buddhas because the falsity is simply the energy of the mind which is in a bit of a spin. You are caught up in the flow of thoughts and you imagine that you are a thought. The whole of samsara is everybody pretending to be like everybody else! None of us are actually who we really are; we are all anxiously looking at one another. The reason we do that is because we are not anybody.

Of course we have the potential to be everything but when we retreat into ourselves then we wonder what shall we be? If we are part of how things are it is obvious what to be; we are what we are. It is in the separation where 'I, me, myself' seems to be something existing. I am me, but who am I? I am like you. I do what you do, but now you are doing what I do. Oh dear, now we are both lost!

We do this because we have lost ourselves and of course the more we copy other people, the more we become alienated from ourselves. Between how we are now and being at home in ourselves, we have got all these thoughts about who we thought we were when we were trying to be who we thought we had to be.

I am very bad at throwing out old clothes since I think I can always wear things a little bit longer. Sometimes it's quite difficult as a therapist when I am sitting in my old shirt and trousers and at the end of the session the patient gives me enough money to buy a new shirt and trousers. They must think they are coming to make a contribution to the Salvation Army! My clothes are old and not very smart but I have an emotional attachment to them. We all have these habits and beliefs inside ourselves about things we used to do. The content of our mind is what stands between ourselves and our own awakening.

When we sit in the meditation, the instruction is just to relax and open and to be with what is there. Let it come – let it go – we don't need it. I don't need this old shirt but I like it. The wardrobe of clothes is bulging and the mind is bulging with its own patterns. *'I am sure it's useful. I haven't worn it for a while but you never know...'* This is attachment. This is your own falsity. You don't need it but you want it just in case you might need it. *'I know I don't need it, but I might need it.'* 'I don't need it' is a fact. 'I might need it' is a fantasy. Fact or fantasy? Fantasy. What Nuden Dorje says is, without changing them, stay open. This goes back to what we were looking at this morning about the one ground and two paths.

The second path is forgetting the ground and then bulging with all this stuff that we have to accept or reject. There is always more to be done yet all the doing is the energy of the mind arising from the mind itself. He is saying in the midst of your confusion — with all your limitations, with your habit formations and your judgement about your habit formations, with your despair about yourself, with your fears of getting old, with everything — just relax and open. These thoughts are the radiance of the mind itself.

Many tribal cultures around the world developed a pattern identified by 19th century European and American anthropologists who named them 'cargo cults'. When tribal people first came into contact with technologically advanced Western people they had often arrived by boat or plane. They would unload many objects from their boats or planes that these tribes had never seen before. The tribes knew nothing about the factories and other places where these things had been made so they acted as if everything just came from the boat or plane. In New Guinea, in Melanesia and in some South American cultures the local people began to chop down trees and make replicas of boats and offer new rituals to the boat, so that the boat would fill itself up with the same kinds of things that the western people's boats had been full of. 'Cargo' refers to all the stuff the boat carries, and 'cult' means the religious orientation that believes it has found the source of the cargo. If they had seen 'cargo' being unloaded from planes they would sometimes build runways for aeroplanes to land. If you are Western then you might think this is a bit crazy, but if you have never seen a factory or known how things are produced then it does make some sense: cargo is something that comes out of the boat or the plane. It is confusion about causes: you think you have found why something is there.

Likewise, we in samsara think our ideas come from our education, our family, our DNA, our diet, from the evolution of the human brain according to the school of Darwin... We have all sorts of ideas about where things came from and so we worship in various kinds of temples like the Temple of Science, the Temple of Education, the Temple of Psychotherapy and so on. But where is the real factory? Where do thoughts come from? Scientists would say from the Good Church of Biochemical Changes in the brain. If you enter that church when you are young and you learn the proper rituals and you get a degree in biology, or train as a doctor, or a PhD in research into neurophysiology, and if you do your prayers every day, then by the time you are thirty-five years old you will have become a professor.

And then there are all these interesting international conferences where you can meet together with ten thousand other worshippers at the Church of the Brain. When you come home you arrive at the airport carrying a little bag advertising the conference you have just attended. You say hello to people whom you know will review your book. You praise and admire them, and they praise and admire you. You review their book, and they review your book. How mutually beneficial is the scientific community! This is how people live; this is a theory of origin.

—*Mummy, where do babies come from?*

—*The stork brings them.*

The stork story is certainly better then thinking about mummy and daddy having sex!

Buddhism is saying that these areas of causation are confusing. Yes, they are very intelligent in building up a basis of evidence and yes, they do have some predictive capacity, but here, now, in this moment, where is the mind?

Relax and open as the clarity of your mind itself and all the thoughts, feelings, doubts, hesitancies and anxieties continue to rise and pass. You don't feel better than you were before but strangely the presence of these formerly disturbing thoughts doesn't cause as much disturbance because they are just moving in space. They are here but they are not defining us; they are just different kinds of things arising and passing.

When you like growing green things, any difference between flowers and weeds is not so important. But when you create a garden that you want your neighbours to approve of, the difference between flowers and weeds is very important. To my eye some flowers are quite boring and not very attractive whereas some weeds are very interesting, but weeds are 'bad' and flowers are 'good'. We don't see what is there; we see them through the category that we use to identify what they are. We tell the growing thing what it is and on the basis of this we pull it out and annihilate it without guilt or shame. We think we have done a good thing because flowers and weeds should not be kept together otherwise the weeds will take over. Garden apartheid is very important. A weed is a flower in the wrong place, some people say.

It is the same in your mind: good thoughts and bad thoughts — you don't want them having sex because you don't know what weird new species is going to evolve! You have to protect this innocent little good thought from a sexy bad thought and all this policing can keep us pretty busy. If you have a garden you need a tool for taking out the weeds. This kind of tool you will find in many kinds of buddhism. Dzogchen, however, is saying that there is one ground and everything is the fruit of the ground. Calling one a flower and another a weed doesn't make any difference; both are just an idea and both are the richness of the earth. Therefore, when you are sitting in meditation, stay open to whatever is arising. Don't try to get rid of some experiences and don't over-privilege other experiences.

THE MIND HAS THREE ASPECTS

The mind has these three aspects: the ground, the field of appearance, and the unique specificity of ourselves moment by moment. Our specificity is in relation to the field or the setting. If we were sitting in a cafe we wouldn't be sitting like we are here now, but because we are in this room exploring some ideas of buddhist teaching many of us are sitting cross-legged. The field, the shared endeavour, how we all are together, creates the conditions by which our bodies take particular postures. Within that our own individuality has us sitting or moving, with our hands still or moving.

These three aspects of ourselves are inseparable. We are the infinite ground of emptiness. We are the complete field as it manifests and we are each this embodied specific being. There is no contradiction between these three aspects.

This is the integration of manifestation in its own ground. But when we are not attentive to the ground or the field then we just have this individual body and we find it difficult to work out how to relate to what is around us: *'If I am this then I am not that, and therefore that is not me. I can know a bit about me, but I am not sure what that is or what that means for me. Are you my friend or my enemy? Will you kiss me or stab me?* This is what we call existential anxiety or ontological insecurity, and is a kind of anxiety or weariness that no amount of thinking will resolve.

Nuden Dorje says that our basic falsity is how we isolate ourselves as someone apart from everything around us. But there is nowhere to go to become more yourself; you are yourself right here. The issue is not about finding yourself. The issue is about finding yourself here in this situation, because this makes you like this. How we are is here. When I am at the airport I am not like this because I am not a thing. There isn't a 'James' who is always James. 'James' is a name which is applied to a whole range of behaviours according to the situation. The individual manifestation is part of the field. The field is the fruit or the showing or the energetic display of unborn emptiness. The place of enlightenment is always here and now.

The dharmakaya – the mind of the Buddha – is not some transcendent function way ahead of you; it is how you are when you recognise the ground of your own being.

Verse 19: Relax, Free of Holding

"Remain relaxed in the unwavering display of this state. If you try to hold on to it with forced recollection then it will be difficult for the natural condition to be self-liberating in its own place. Keep recollection and awareness in the fresh state of natural occurrence, estate three of strong grasping."

'**Remain relaxed in the unwavering display of this state.**' This means manifestation continues coming and nobody knows how it is going to be; it just is as it is. However the mind is, stay relaxed and open.

Control is our biggest fantasy. The new Pope wants to reform the Catholic Church, and we wish him well as it is not going to be easy. When Obama became President everybody had a lot of hope, but the Senate and the Congress were against him so he was not able to do very much. The Dalai Lama, with all his intelligence and charm, has not managed to change Chinese policy on Tibet. In Tibetan Buddhism many people believe that the Karmapa is a very high and powerful incarnation, but he found it very difficult to get a visa to come to the West. The reason for saying these things is to understand that we are like children who want to have Santa Claus. '*My daddy is big and powerful, and he can do anything.*' But all these big papas have limitations because we look at them through the wrong paradigm.

The fantasy is that if you have enough power you can control everything. Napoleon, the great conqueror and leader, was trapped by the Russian snow. The army of Adolf Hitler froze at Stalingrad. These grand powers with the frightening capacity to impact the lives of others eventually turn to dust. Power is a very false god. Tenderness, collaboration and helpfulness is much more important. People working together. Sitting in the meditation and collaborating with your own mind, not trying to control what sort of thoughts arise, since this is impossible anyway. Thoughts come because they come.

None of us know exactly what kind of karma we have behind us. I remember when my teacher was explaining karma to me he said it's like a very long train. All the actions that you do in this life are put into one carriage and this is hooked on to the end of the train, so when the train comes round the mountain, behind the engine, you have the first carriage. The first carriage contains very old karma and you don't know what is in it. *'I have been a good person – I did this and that – so I don't deserve this bad luck.'* This is not to understand karma because what you get is from way back. This is what he explained to me.

Nowadays when you go to buy food in the shops it has a 'sell by' or 'use by' date stamped on it. But when you do an action it gets stamped with a 'forget by' date! There are many things we done in our lives that we cannot remember, but they don't forget us; they are back at the end of the long train. Sooner or later it comes and gets delivered to us and then we find ourselves being sick, or having difficulties with family, or living in a time and place of war and famine.

When I first arrived in India I was very lucky to meet many famous high lamas. They were amazing meditators with many powers and we learned all about their histories and lineages. But they also had another name – refugee –, which is not so powerful. Therefore, it is important not to be seduced by the idea of power, dominance and control. Control means: subject dominating object. However when you win, you also lose. If you win you make enemies. It is the same in the meditation practice; it is not about being rough, tough or powerful. Sometimes we may do practices like *chöd* and so on for cutting and shaping the pattern of experience, but that is not the main function. The main function is awakening to the natural or the given integration of these three aspects of our existence: unborn open space; the radiant field of experience; and our specific manifestation moment by moment.

This is how it is – you don't have to make it – you just have to not ignore it. You don't need anything rough to make it happen and when you get it you haven't got to do anything. You don't need to sit on a throne and wear a fancy hat. You are not better than other people. The royal path is invisibility. Imagine if you were the Queen of England. You are on the stage twenty-four hours a day. Likewise with the Pope, the Karmapa or the Dalai Lama. They have no private life. When you win you also lose.

We are very lucky because we can be sad, depressed, go to the shops, whatever. No one cares what we do. There is a lot of freedom in being ordinary. You have the freedom to know that today you are unhappy or jealous, whereas the Queen of England has to pretend that everything is fine. When a swan moves serenely across the water, we know that underneath the water the swan's big black feet are paddling very fast, but the swan appears to be gliding very gracefully. Humans swim more like a dog splashing about and some days are happy and other days are sad. What does this mean? It means that some days I am happy and some days I am sad. But why? Who knows? Who cares? If I am sad, I am sad. If I am thirsty, I have a drink. If I need to have a pee, I go to the toilet. It is just like that.

This is what the teachings say about the life of the yogi. Sleep when you are tired and eat when you are hungry. It is all very simple.

—I am upset.

—I thought you practised meditation, so you shouldn't be upset.

—No, actually before I practised meditation I couldn't be upset and now I can be upset because I know everything is impermanent, and so I am upset for a while.

—But you're upset!

—Don't pin that on me. I am upset, but the fact that you know I am upset doesn't mean that I am upset because what 'upset 'means for you and how I experience it is not the same.

This is very important for us because then we can be free to feel what we feel and to stop pretending, and then we get free of our own falsity.

For many years I lived in a room at the back of my guru's house in India. Every now and then he would walk around the little garden and come to see how I was doing. If I was lying on my bed in that little room and I heard his footsteps, because there were many bits of trees that had fallen down and he would crunch on the branches, I would jump up. Look at me, see how I am a good boy, always working! Fucking crazy! Worrying about what someone else will think. Cheating me and cheating him. And of course he knew.

Again and again the key thing we need to watch for is rigidity, reification, and objectification; making aspects of ourselves strongly real. The more we allow ourselves to be the way we are, the more we see that this current formation is just a manifestation, a showing, but it doesn't show who I really am. The mirror shows many different reflections yet the content of none of these reflections shows what the mirror really is. What they show is the capacity of the mirror to show.

When you feel confused or lost or unhappy or intelligent, or clear and competent – whatever it is – this shows the creative potential and the richness of the mind; it doesn't show or define you. No matter how I am, this is not **who** I am, so now I can say, *'This is how I am today.'* The fact that you see me looking sad means that I look sad. You don't know anything about me except, *'Today James looks sad.'* It doesn't mean anything about how James will be tomorrow because the sadness is not definitive of James.

This is the paradoxical freedom of non-duality. The more you fully are how you are, the less you are caught by how you are. This is wonderful because you don't have to manage or edit or shape yourself according to any map in your head.

STOP TRYING TO GRASP THE WATERFALL

'If you try to hold on to it with forced recollection then it will be difficult for the natural condition to be self-liberating in its own place.' The thought is arising and it's a bit dull, exciting, or confusing. You're a bit too close to the thought. *'My mind shouldn't be this way. I am going to make it clear.'* You start trying to get rid of this particular mood or flavour that you are caught up in.

Nuden Dorje is saying that is artificial because you are making an effort; you are not trusting how it is. Although the thoughts, feelings and sensations are arising and passing like the waves coming in and out of the ocean you are fixating on the shape of a particular wave, thinking it isn't quite right, and your very arousal into changing the wave blocks you from seeing that the wave goes free by itself. Everything goes free by itself, therefore, I don't need to do anything. The ego has less and less responsibility and so you really relax and are part of the movement of the co-emergent field. As long as you situate apart from what is occurring and make judgments about it, and try to change it, your own attempt to help will be the cause of harm.

'Keep recollection and awareness in the fresh state of natural occurrence, the state free of strong grasping.'

The Tibetan term used in this line is *rang bab* which means falling by itself, or like a waterfall tumbling down a mountain.

The water is falling and sometimes the wind blows and moves it a little bit – it comes as it comes. He is saying that if you allow yourself to be present with however the mind is coming everything is shown to you so you don't need to grasp. You can't grasp the waterfall as the water is going by. The flow of experience is unceasing. No matter how quick you are at grasping you won't catch the water. What you might catch is an idea; something moving in the flow, but when you catch the idea you also find that it is not there. *'Ah! Now I understand.'* That is a thought and then it's gone; it is always going.

The content, the field and the ground are together. Because we are used to being an isolated individual we think that the content of the mind is the most important thing — *What thoughts are arising for us? What are we thinking? What are we planning?* — but all of these as phenomena are vanishing. Nuden Dorje is telling us not to try to hold on to anything because we never get anything. If we trust something new will arise we will be there and able to respond.

In that sense we move from being a settled farmer to being a nomad. The nomad takes the sheep, the goats, and the cattle up to the high plains in the summer where there is grass, but the farmer, down in the plains, has to wait and hope that the rain will come.

Go where the grass is; be where it is rather than saying, *'This is where I stay. I'll put a wall around my field because it is my field. It may be full of weeds but it's my field.'* That is not so useful.

Verse 20: Eat the soup

The actual ground and the false ground

'If you awaken to the falsity of your confused existence, you are buddha free of ground and root.'

We have the actual ground and the false ground as Nuden Dorje has been showing us in many ways.

The actual ground of our experience is the spacious awareness of the mind.

The false ground is 'I, me, myself.' Who are you? *'I am just me. I have always been me.'* This feels like something quite stable: because I am me this is what I do. What I do seems to be like a plant growing out of the ground of 'me' spreading out like a root with a stalk and a flower. *'I do this because I am me, and I am me because I do this.'* Buddhism calls this stupidity, nevertheless it is what we believe: my activities are a mirror that show me myself, and I reveal my activities to myself. This is the false ground constructed out of concept and memory. It is a formulation forming itself by investment and it requires us to keep maintaining it for the very reason that it is false.

The natural state, the actual ground, is not false. If we awaken to how we are false, and if we stop indulging the falsity, it is obvious how it is. The only reason we didn't feel at home in 'how it is' is because we were trying to be something else. 'How it is' is what is called buddha.

Verse 21: Get the Point

'There is no other way but to understand yourself. Recognising your mind as Samantabhadra you will see your own face. If this is not directly experienced you will be confused by wrong thoughts and will identify yourself with whatever confused thoughts arise.

Going on pilgrimage to Mount Kailash or building a stupa won't make you enlightened. Offering lots of money to some important lama or doing lots of mantras won't make you enlightened. We have to understand why. Because there are two aspects: stillness and movement.

It is like a dirty movement and holy movement. Dirty movement involves cheating and lying and spending your life trying to make money and so on. This is a worldly movement and it just goes round and round in circles. However you are now embarking on a holy sacred movement. You make prostrations, you learn to construct a mandala and you visualise many things; these are all movements of the mind. They are holy but they are movement and movement is not the same as stillness. If you want to be still, then doing movement won't get you there. If you want to find stillness, stop identifying with movement.

'But this is a very important movement. My lama said if I do a million mantras I will be enlightened.' How? Mantra is all movement. The breath is going in and out, the throat is going up and down and vibration is being sent in the air. Movement influences other movement. The world is made of movement. When you move in a useful way it impacts the field of movement and you get good results coming. This is called compassion. Compassion is not the same as wisdom since wisdom is understanding the basis of movement. When you are moving you don't recognise that you are moving, you are just doing what has to be done.

If you want to understand the nature of stillness you have to relax. When the bus comes, don't get on it, don't even get on a bicycle! Thoughts and feelings are arising and then they are gone. You didn't move – the thought moved. The bus is always going through the still quiet land. Stillness and movement are not fundamentally in opposition but by making effort and trying to change and do things you are in the house of movement. It is not very complicated or difficult to understand.

There are many kinds of meditation practices and you have to understand what their individual functions are. In the Tibetan tradition there are many pujas or ritual visualisation systems with offerings. The general name for them is *trinle* which means movement or activity. Reciting a mantra is an activity because the mind is visualising something, the mouth is saying something, and the fingers are flicking the mala beads round and round. However in dzogchen our goal is to relax into natural unborn awareness, and there is no method to do this since it is done by not doing.

This is sometimes called *gom med gom* the meditation of non-meditation. We are not trying to achieve anything. In many kinds of meditation you know exactly what you are going to do even before you sit down because you know what the object or the focus of that particular practice is beforehand. '*I am going to focus on my breath, or I am going to focus on visualising Padmasambhava.*' But in dzogchen practice we focus on whatever arises; we have nothing to prepare in advance. Whatever comes, I am here too. I am in the gang. Is that what we are doing? Okay. Whatever happens, we are here, so it doesn't matter what happens. It is the being here-ness that is the key.

How are we going to be here? The mind is always here because without the mind we wouldn't be here. We are already here. How do we find ourselves being here? By not getting on the bus. The bus doesn't go here; it goes from here to there. It is that simple. Don't get on the bus – don't merge in the thought – don't push the thought away. Merging and rejecting are two forms of movement: pushing in and pulling away.

Right from the very beginning the mind is here. We are here. We are not dead. This is the mind. Experience is coming and going, moving and changing moment by moment. This is movement within the space of the mind. To find the space of the mind relax the identification with movement. Don't do anything. Just trust it is okay and that there is nothing to do. Of course, that is quite hard because our ego identity is made out of movement.

Before the break we looked at what happened for steelworkers and miners when factories and mines closed down. Losing your job is linked to losing your identity. When we do the meditation and there is nothing for you to do, so you start to feel the shimmering anxiety at the root of the ego. This is the impulse that takes us back into identification and the movement of the mind. Again and again we enter the practice and relax, and continue to relax in the face of all the urges and the impulses to get involved. Nuden Dorje is saying that there is no other way to understand yourself; it is your mind which is the site of enlightenment

The teaching on dzogchen is different from that of other systems. There are many paths to enlightenment that involve transforming samsara into nirvana. But in the dzogchen teaching it says that you can have a piece of coal and even if you wash it for years and years, it will still be black. Coal doesn't have the nature of chalk; it is black and doesn't become white by washing. Likewise the ego doesn't have the nature of enlightenment. You, as ego, will never be enlightened. But don't worry. Your mind is already enlightened. Instead of trying to make the ego enlightened, which no-one can ever do, it is better to be where the light is. People can spend a lot of time trying to improve themselves. Fifty years of self-improvement may be followed by dementia; all the self-improvement is washed away. All of our activity is like sandcastles. The tide comes in and the construction is washed away. You cannot construct enlightenment.

In this tradition they say *ye-ne sang-ye*. Buddhahood (*sang-ye*) is there from the very beginning (*ye-ne*) by itself. That is what buddha nature is. It doesn't need to be improved, it just needs to be allowed to be what it is, so don't falsify it by trying to improve something which is already completed. The mind itself is dzogpa chenpo – complete. But maybe a few flowers around the edge would be nice? Or perhaps we could just add a little of this very nice perfume? Not necessary. All that is required of us is that we relax and become who we already are.

'Recognising your mind as Samantabhadra, you will see your own face.' The meaning of the word 'Samantabhadra' is 'always good.' It refers to two aspects: the mind and the content of the mind. The content of the mind is changing and as we know sometimes it is shit and it doesn't feel very nice to be ourselves. So how do we recognise that our nature is always good? The 'always good' is the mind which is always open. The mirror is 'always good,' even though the reflection may be good, bad, ugly, beautiful or whatever. The qualities of the reflection don't alter the nature of the mirror.

On a good day you may feel relaxed and friendly and want to be with people, but on a bad day you may want to stay at home and not answer the phone. This is the content of the mind; it doesn't alter the open nature of the mind. The mind is the hospitality that allows you the privilege of having a bad day; worries are admitted. In this restaurant we can bring in children, dogs, cats, whatever we like. Seeing that our nature is always good means opening to the unborn mind itself. To fixate on the content of the mind, for instance, *'Oh, my back is sore,'* is sensation and the conceptual apprehension of the sensation. Both will change with time.

In dzogchen practice the mind is still open but doesn't get caught up in the content. We allow whatever comes to come, and whatever goes to go. This is the actuality of our existence.

'If this is not directly experienced you will be confused by wrong thoughts and will identify yourself with whatever confused thoughts arise.' I have not translated this very literally since what I translate as 'If this is not directly experienced' in Tibetan is more like 'if this is not realised'. But the word 'realise' means to make real, and real means substantial. Therefore, I don't think that 'realised' is a helpful word for us. However 'experience' is also a bit difficult because it has the sense of 'I will experience this.' Have you experienced the amazing fragrance of the orange blossom trees here in Aracena? Earlier we were walking down from the citadel and entered a square and suddenly we experienced this incredible perfume.

We don't experience our mind in the same way. I don't know any language where I could describe this accurately, so I am moved more and more towards an ontological language. It is more like, 'if you don't allow yourself to be as you are,' but being is not like in 'being a good student'. Instead of saying 'Be natural!', you just find yourself being natural by not over-stimulating yourself. You relax into just playing, just playing in the way you can see the lovely children playing in the square. That is what is implied here – allow yourself just to relax into it. It is not even like 'allowing' since in allowing there is a giving up of effort. Simply stop struggling. No struggle, no pain, no effort.

'If you don't really just relax and open into this you will be confused by wrong thoughts and identify yourself with whatever confused thoughts arise.' We have two options: either we merge with thoughts or we relax in the spaciousness through which all these thoughts and feelings arise. In the second, space and the movement are now integrated. We can still go to work or drive a car, but we are not trying to work out what has to be done. We are not relying on thoughts for meaning and so thoughts are no longer being perverted from their actual function, which is to be communicative as an aspect of compassion. Again and again, Nuden Dorje makes the point that we have to keep relaxing because every time we are self-forgetful we will be in this matrix of self-constitution as something.

Verse 22: Busy being lost

'With reliance on notions of 'I' and 'me,' all phenomena whether outer (in the world), or inner (in the mind), or fixed (like the sky or the earth), or moving (rivers, waterfalls), everything that appears are perceived to be existing as real entities. Each thing is named and labelled and its qualities are enumerated.'

If I am drunk, and I don't stop drinking, I will continue to be drunk. In order to stop being drunk what I have to do is stop drinking. If I am drunk on thoughts on the basis of that, everything is real and I am drunk with the impact of these many different things. 'Intoxicated' means toxic. We are poisoned by this false belief about the true, separate, substantial existence of myself and all other phenomena. If we want the symptoms of toxicity to be resolved we have to stop taking the poison. The difficulty with this is that we think the toxic substance is medicine.

If we have this belief in the true existence of things then, **'Each thing is named and labelled and its qualities are enumerated.'** Our capacity to know what things are and make distinctions is our intelligence, so this is a very challenging notion. It is saying that we are intoxicated and poisoned by our own intelligence which misapprehends how things are.

In English, we have a saying, *'You can know the price of everything but the value of nothing.'* Nuden Dorje is saying that we can know the price, we can put the name, we can evaluate it and give all sorts of ratings, but we lack the aesthetic appreciation to really value what is occurring because what things actually are, is the radiance of the buddha mind.

Verse 23: Just a Pinball

'Whatever appears is taken to be a variety of external objects. 'These are then evaluated and held to be truly existing. Subtle and insistent thoughts keep occurring and we follow after whatever arises, whatever we recollect.'

When we look out of the window we see houses, people, trees, cars and so on, and they appear to be strongly real for us. The car doesn't call itself a car. It is us who say that this is a car. We are naming and labelling all of these things. The substance, the essence, of all of these phenomena is in our own mind. When we don't recognise this we are stuck as a thing in a world of things.

As soon as we apprehend something, to remove the terror of the 'something-ness' of the world, which is quite shocking, we tame and domesticate it by incorporating it into a narrative. *'The houses here are really nice. They are a bit like the ones in the next village. Have you been there? It's really pretty.'* On, and on, and on. The Japanese are incredibly good at wrapping up presents with beautiful paper and exquisite bows, and this is what we do with our stories. We wrap every aspect up inside them and by doing this it makes all this weird stuff less strange.

In the development of European literature there were the so-called Gothic novels which included books such as Frankenstein by Mary Shelley, and Dracula by Bram Stoker. This was a kind of shadow reaction to the modernist cult of industrialisation — a 'return of the repressed' whereby what you make will not stay the way you made it, but will take on a life of its own, like in The Nutcracker ballet. It gives us a sense of the strangeness of the world. Are we sure that things are what we take them to be? Our unease makes us want to wrap more and more narrative around them otherwise how do we live?

When the Germans invaded France and Marshal Pétain set up the Vichy government, there were various small resistance movements, but many people collaborated and parallel governments were set up. Towards the middle period of the war, General Charles de Gaulle was living in London and he tried to organise the various resistance movements in France. After there had been the allied landing of mainly American and British troops through Normandy – the so-called Liberation of France – there came the day of the liberation of Paris. The French troops led the way – not many of them – but they were at the front, and at the front of the French troops was General Charles de Gaulle – the liberator of France – and he gave a speech, beginning with words to the effect that France had been liberated by the French. If you ever watch Hollywood movies then you know this is not quite true. It was not quite true that the French had been united in their struggle for freedom. History was rewritten so that at the end of the war their national dignity survived intact.

Who needs truth when you can have a good story? This is the world of the ego. All kinds of terrible things were covered up. People who were big associates of the Germans were back in the French government; they reinvented themselves. This is the play of signifiers. This is the way we can cheat ourselves because the ego needs to feel in charge of all this stuff. If the French had had to think that half the country had been Nazi then there could have been civil war with people being murdered and all the rest of it, so better to smooth it over. There are some similar stories here in Spain. We, human beings, cannot bear too much reality.

Meditation is important because it is not trying to establish the truth through concentration and differing opinions and views. As Nuden Dorje says, subtle and insistent thoughts keep occurring and we follow them and they create our world. There are all kinds of different histories of the last hundred years in Spain, France, Britain and Germany. Right-wing historians, liberal historians, communist historians, and so on. There is no end to this development of stories.

Relax and open. The clarity of the mind is like the depth of the ocean and stories are like the waves on the surface. This is important for us because our world is so very amazing. It is now possible with satellite television to see many different news broadcasting companies. I sometimes watch the Russian or French news and they are completely different from the British version of the news. Then if I look at Al Jazeera, once again it is completely different. News is like the Tower of Babel. What can you believe?

In dzogchen they say you don't have to believe stories. The truth is not going to be established through stories. There is no dogma to believe and uphold. Stop struggling, stop creating, stop being busy. Allow yourself to see the flow of experience. The one who sees the flow of experience is the eye of the Buddha; not looking at experience from a distance, but seeing by being present in the moment of the unfolding of experience.

Day Four

Meditation practice

VERSE 24: THE FAULT OF FOCUSSING ON OBJECTS

'Some people try to make use of confusion to cut the root of confusion. They believe in the existence of that which does not exist and think that an understanding of the signification of the objects is very important. This is the way not to do practice, this is the way not to see the faults in your meditation.'

DON'T ASK THOUGHTS TO DO WHAT THOUGHTS CAN'T DO

This verse is a criticism of an analytical approach to practice. By memorising a lot of buddhist categories we can make very fine distinctions about different kinds of phenomena. Nuden Dorje is saying here that this is just another flavour of confusion because we are taking names and categories to be of primary significance, but they are not. The more we gain the confidence that we can understand what is going on by relying on concepts the more we create a prison of gold. Whether the prison is made of gold or of stone you are still trapped.

Words and concepts tell us about the domain of words and concepts. In themselves they are not bad or wrong but if we ask them to do what they can't do then we will be confused and disappointed.

'This is the way not to do practice, this is the way not to see the faults in your meditation.' When we meditate many different experiences arise. Sometimes the mind is very dull and heavy and sometimes it is very busy with a continuous stream of thoughts and we jump from one thought to another. Or it might be full of angry thoughts about problems at work. We might find that there are thoughts and feelings about somebody you miss who is far away. As we know many, many different things can happen.

The point being made here is not to go analysing what kind of problem you have. If you feel depressed you don't need to go on the Internet and read about depression. The issue is not to know more about the object formation but to relax identification with the secondary thought form which arises and says, *'Oh, I feel bad.'* Stay with the actual experiencer. Here we are in this room together and each of us is having a stream of experiences occurring. Who is the experiencer?

This is like the Zen koan: Show me the face you had before you were born. When we think about what is happening for us we show our 'second order' face; the face we have developed through our education and learning. Each of us can say hundreds of things about this room: the shape, the colour, the lighting, the windows and so on. When we behave in this way — analysing and connecting — the answer to the question *'Who is the experiencer of this room?'* is very clear. *'I am the experiencer of this room. If you don't believe me I can tell you all about the room.'* This is what is dangerous, says Nuden Dorje.

By relying on our capacity to build up these interpretive pictures we imagine that we are describing something out there, but there is a secret implicit activity that is confirming our own individual status as the 'knower' or the 'doer,' whether we are talking about the room or about experiences in meditation.

Relax the busy mind — we don't need this conceptual elaboration. If you want to find the experiencer don't tell yourself who this is, but relax, open and see.

The experiencer is the clarity of space. This is the experiencing as showing, and within the field of showing there is the line of knowing.

We are here in the room and the room is showing itself. I can count one, two, three pillars in the room. The narrative I can develop about features of the room is simply another line of movement moving in the sphere of display which shows the room. It is not that me, sitting here, is talking about the room over there, but the room includes me and my thoughts and talking about it. Everything that occurs is the display of the clarity of the mind.

As we looked before, duality means the separation of subject and object and we can endlessly refine the details about what is the object and what is the subject. But when we relax and are present, what we call subject and object are both clearly movements within the radiant expanse of the mind.

Whenever you feel that your mind is heavy and dull or overexcited, or you feel that you can't meditate, then just relax and allow what is here to be here. We become upset because we don't want our mind to be sad or depressed or excited, but if that is how it is, your mind is still there. If you didn't have a mind you wouldn't be bored. It is the mind of the Buddha which shows the thought, *'I don't know how to meditate – this is a waste of time.'* Somebody is aware of the thought *'I can't do this',* so rather than focussing on the semantic content of the thought just bring your presence, awareness and attention to the point where this thought is arising.

As we have looked before, don't merge into the thought. Don't believe it, don't trust it, don't try to avoid it or get away from it as if it were something dangerous or disgusting; just relax and open to the presence of the thoughts. When you relax you see the thoughts go and gradually, like the arising of the dawn in the dark of the night, you start to see that the mind is not moving, but that these experiences are moving. This is the one antidote to all these problems.

In my book, *SIMPLY BEING*, are two chapters which focus specifically on meditation problems. They give many examples of the different kinds of difficulties that can arise but always with the same solution: don't avoid the thought; don't believe the thought; don't fall into it; stay present as the thought is arising. That very presence is the complexion or the radiance of the mind itself.

Maybe we all like to feel that we are special and that we have our own special difficulties that other people don't quite understand, but actually how the mind functions is very transparent. How we get lost is easy to see – it's just getting lost – there is no need for blame or shame and it's not a sign that you are stupid or bad or have bad karma; it is just you have to be there where it's happening.

If you find that you are very distracted then maybe go for a run around the block or have a shower. When you feel a bit more tired just relax and go into the practice. The most important thing is not to struggle. The one who struggles is the ego, and if you are sitting in the place of the ego that is what you will find. Struggle will only give you more of your familiar personality structures. Relax – it's already there – allow it to show itself.

Verse 25: The Great Completion

'When thoughts about the immutable nature arise, remain relaxed without doing anything artificial. Mind itself abides in its own nature whatever arises. Neither wait expectantly for what might come nor seek to follow what has gone. Abide in the ever-fresh state of the primordially pure present awareness.'

If you have thoughts that you don't understand this, or that seem completely strange or stupid, or if you start to think that your meditation is very good and that now you finally understand — when thoughts like that come they are just thoughts. The thought is a bus and you don't need to get on the bus. Whether the bus is going to 'Sad Land' or to 'Happy Land,' you just keep sitting on the bench in the park.

Thoughts always vanish. The thought is always a thought about something; it is not the mind itself. Don't focus on the thought, as the text says, **remain relaxed without doing anything artificial**. Allow all these experiences to arise and pass away. Life goes on. If the answer was a thought, how would you keep it? Maybe you could have it tattooed on your forehead and then you could look in the mirror and think, *'Oh, Wow! I'm a buddha.'* Thoughts vanish. Good and bad experiences come and go. The mirror is there whatever kind of reflections are coming, so no need to hold onto thoughts or push them away.

'Mind itself abides in its own nature whatever arises.' This means that the key thing is the spacious awareness. This is more important than any thought, feeling, or sensation because this awareness is unchanging.

'Neither wait expectantly for what might come nor seek to follow what has gone.' This is the true diagnostic test. People come to buddhist teachings like this because they feel that something is not

quite right. They don't feel complete; something is lacking in life. What is lacking? We want something to fill us. We want to hang on to some good events. We have memories of ourselves. Many people have photos of their children or someone they love on their screensaver or in their wallet. *'When I see the picture it reminds me of who I am.'*

But my thoughts, my memories, what I have done in my life, have gone. They have wandered off into the past. Every now and then they send you a postcard and you remember something. What the postcard says is, *'Having a good time. Glad you are not here.'* The past is the past and the future hasn't come. Looking forward to something which is not here, or missing something which has gone, are methods of not being here. What you get from the future or the past are mirages or ghosts; they don't fill you. In fact we don't need something to fill us. The lack or the gap that we feel is the lack of not being in touch with what we do have. The mind itself is the great completion: it is whole and full and its quality is satisfaction.

THE INFINITY OF THE PRESENT MOMENT

In this openness of the mind, if happy events come we can laugh, and if sad events come we can cry; it is not about staying in some homogenised state. We know that happiness and sadness will pass and that this is not the real thing. This is just the display – the movement – so gather yourself into the infinity of the present moment because of course the past and the future are here in the present. All we ever have is now and this now is infinite; it's big and it contains everything.

He says: **'Abide in the ever fresh state of the primordially pure present awareness.'** Relax and trust that openness will give you whatever you need.

Verse 26: Abide Naturally

'The flow of confusing thoughts cannot be stopped, just like the wind or a waterfall in the mountains. Therefore towards whatever arises, however it arises, maintain the natural state of open awareness.'

This great yogi, Nuden Dorje, was a master of meditation and even he is saying that confusing thoughts are always there. It gives us a lot of hope. It is not that we arrive at a time when everything is washed clean. We don't get rid of confusing thoughts; the key thing is not to be troubled by them.

I was born in 1949, just a few years after the end of the Second World War, and in the house I grew up in my mother continued the habits from the war. In Britain the war meant rationing and this continued until 1954. There was not much in the shops, so we didn't throw anything away. As a child this was wonderful because when I opened a little cupboard there were endless piles of string. When my mother came back from the shops she would take the shopping out of their paper bags, flatten and fold the bags and put them in another little drawer. My father would get a bit irritated. My mother would say, *'But you never know when they will be useful.'* It is the same with all these thoughts which arise in the mind. When they go out of your mind they are still floating around someplace and when you need them they come back. We don't need them just now so we put them away. If my mother had kept all the string and the paper bags out on the table there would have been no place to eat; so we let things go, but they don't vanish.

This is a strange thing. The more you allow your thoughts to go free, the more your mind becomes bright and sharp. We probably all know what it's like to worry. When we worry, like a goat tied to a stick by a rope, it keeps going round and round and round. When we worry we go over the same material again and again but it doesn't help us progress or make us more intelligent. By sleeping on it, the next morning we might find a solution. We have probably all found this to be true. When you let it go somehow it moves in space and you see it differently.

So the text says not to struggle – just let the river flow and the wind blow. On a windy day you can see that the clouds are moving very fast. Things push other things. Thoughts chase thoughts through the space of the mind, but they don't catch the space. Therefore by being open and spacious you don't have to block or direct the thoughts. **'Therefore towards whatever arises, however it arises, maintain the natural state of open awareness.'**

Verse 27: Confusion Resolves Itself

'When one can abide in one's own place free of confusion it is like a river flowing back into the ocean. Thoughts subside in their own place so there is no need to seek smart solutions.'

When you watch a big river you see the inevitability of it reaching the sea. It seems to flow without making any effort. In the same way, if you trust the openness of your mind and return to this again and again, you find you become more spacious, in the same way that the river opens out into the ocean.

'Thoughts subside in their own place so there is no need to seek smart solutions.' Thoughts are self-liberating – they just go.

In the springtime the gardener doesn't have to go and glue little leaves on each branch of the tree. And in the autumn he doesn't have to go up a ladder with some scissors and cut each leaf off. The leaves fall off by themselves. Thoughts go by themselves so you don't need to do anything fancy or to work hard. Trusting this is very important. More happens the less you do.

When you are doing a lot you don't see so much. If you sit on a train as it moves across the countryside you see houses, trees and cows. If you are cycling across a country lane you see a house, a tree or a cow in more detail. When you walk along the path you can stop and really see the house, the tree and the cow. By going slowly, you get more. The world shows more detail to you. When you are running around in an agitated state, although you get a lot, what do you get? You didn't really taste it. You just got the surface as there was no time for the full flavour to unfold.

VERSE 28: ALWAYS ALREADY PRESENT

'Without a ground (ignorance) and devoid of any roots of the five poisons (kleshas) the natural condition is itself empty. Clarity and emptiness are merged as the non-artificial quality of awareness.'

It is empty as it is, and what arises doesn't remove its emptiness. Again, to take the example of the mirror, the mirror shows reflections because it is empty. When we look at the mirror it seems to be full of reflections and yet even when the reflection is there the mirror is empty because its nature is empty.

Another example: here is a glass with water in it. We could say that the glass is almost full of water, but the glass itself is empty and that is why water is inside it. The water is sitting in the emptiness of the glass. The water doesn't remove the emptiness. The glass may be full of water yet still be empty, in its glass-ness. This might seem a contradiction, however the emptiness of the glass is not destroyed or removed by the water. You can take out the water and can put in orange juice instead, or whatever you like. The potential of the glass to be filled with other substances is its basic hospitality and space, and that nature or quality is not removed by the fact that at the moment it has water in it.

CONTRASTING PAPER OR CANVAS WITH MIRROR

If you have a canvas and you paint something on it, although you may paint over the first painting, the basic potential of a blank canvas has been diminished. The space or the potential of a blank canvas is not the same as the space or potential of a mirror. The canvas remains marked when you make a mark on it. The mirror is not marked by the reflection because you can turn the mirror and a whole new reflection enters in or rises out, but somehow it is there.

This is a very important principle as a lot of the time we feel like the canvas. The ego is like canvas. As a person we are marked by the events of our life; we are written on over and over again. We carry the tracings of past writings in our posture, in our tone of voice, in our memories and so on. We are inscribed by our parents and schools and these narratives and messages shape us and are difficult to get rid of. You can go to therapy for many years and still not get free of them.

This is the nature of the ego: the ego is markable, but the mind is not. The ego is an aspect of the mind; the mind is not a possession of the ego. This is very important. Returning to the freshness of the mind is always possible no matter what has happened in your life. What makes it difficult is that we glue ourselves to our narrative. *'I am what happened to me and therefore these marks are important.'* In this way, you, yourself, volunteer to be paper and the self-liberating space of the mirror-like mind is covered over. Of course, it is not really covered over because even the paper is a reflection in the mirror!

'Clarity and emptiness are merged as the non-artificial quality of awareness.' This is precisely the quality of the mirror. The mirror has clarity in its capacity to show yet it is empty at the same time. We have more access to the world through awareness than through the cogitation of our reflective intelligence.

Verse 29: Give it a Rest

'Keeping to the nature of whatever arises there is relaxation free of grasping. If your mind becomes steady you don't have to maintain this with meditation. Remain free of encouraging or inhibiting, stability or movement.'

What is the nature of whatever arises? One way to think about this is to ask what it is that you want to consider. Consider my watch, for example. The quality of the watch is a combination of metal and glass. I use the watch as a method for telling the time, and there are many more things I can say about it. This is our ordinary way of establishing the nature of what happens. The word 'watch' establishes this as a seemingly self-existing phenomenon, and then by saying things about it we get to know it. This is the path of ordinary knowledge. Each phenomenon has its own qualities. Therefore, you need to spend a lot of time learning about all the different things in the world. However that is not what is being referred to here.

The nature of whatever arises is emptiness and clarity. The watch itself has no essence or substance. If you have a hammer you can very easily break up the watch into parts. The watch continues its existence due to the factors of maintenance and these factors will stop at a certain point and the watch will stop working; or I will lose it; or something else happens. But while the factors of maintenance are here it seems to be 'our' watch and, in particular, 'my' watch. As 'my' watch I can tell you the story of how and where and when I bought it; I am filling the watch with a narrative that is artificial. The nature of how the watch is in itself is an appearance which is empty of substance.

If we take the back of the watch we can see all these little wheels operating together. If we had a big microscope we could look inside this pillar that is holding up the hall ceiling and we see the molecules.

On one level the pillar looks stable, but it is a stability generated out of habitual repetitions of movement. The nature of all phenomena is emptiness. When we seek to know what something is we are putting the essence into the object. Sometimes that is very important to do as without it we wouldn't have communication.

COMPASSION IS COMMUNICATION

There are wonderful developments in modern medicine, developed in laboratories sometimes by surgeons. Attention to detail and the precise naming of what is going on is very helpful in the realm of compassion. Compassion is communication. Surgeons are developing new kinds of artificial hip joints for older people made out of metal, steel and plastic, and this is a very useful application of artificiality. Art, and the creativity that develops new forms, is wonderful because it shows the function of forms. There is a lot of research now around how long artificial knee and hip joints will last. This is the quality of the object as object but the nature of the object is empty. It is a composition bringing together different kinds of molecules bonding into a particular shape for a particular purpose.

The fact that everything is empty doesn't mean that it all has one flattened appearance. All the details of the world and the marvels of modern engineering are there but all are empty of essence and substance; they arise from people collaborating together. The designer tests a prototype and if the outcome is good they move it to production. Production informs marketing, so there is communication. Something is produced and what is produced is a form of emptiness.

Meditation won't make the world completely dead to you. In fact you get more details the more relaxed and open your mind is; the detail and the emptiness are inseparable. The problem is in how we apprehend the details. When we invest value in an appearance the function of the appearance is misinterpreted to create the illusion that there is some true essence or substance inside the appearance which is the site of the value.

Another example: my spectacles. I might think these are a really good pair of glasses because I can put the arms up or down, and when I travel around this is incredibly useful, but this is secondary to the fact that the glasses help me to see. The more I like my glasses the more I start to imagine that there is something there. Of course there is something there, but what is its status in being here? The glasses are a meeting place of the glass, the plastic, and the metal joint, and the function of aiding ageing eyes to see clearly. There is no enduring essence to this. I bought these ones when an arm came off the previous pair of glasses I had. It is impermanent and a juxtaposition and each part is a juxtaposition of other smaller parts... ad infinitum.

In general, buddhist texts spend a lot of time talking about impermanence and the compounded nature of phenomena and that is very helpful for understanding this point.

However things may appear, stay relaxed and open to them; the nature of the appearance is empty, so in working with the appearance don't forget the emptiness. As it says in THE HEART SUTRA: form is emptiness; emptiness is form. The fact that the nature of the glasses is empty doesn't get in the way of their function. The fact that they function doesn't make them strongly real in the sense of having an internal definition. Before my eyes got weaker I didn't need to use glasses, and the fact that I have these glasses in my hand now has to do with the change in the muscles in my eyes; due to causes and conditions this arises.

THE ACTIVITY OF FORGETTING

'**If your mind becomes steady you don't have to maintain this with meditation.**' By meditation it means sitting down to do meditation. If the function of the meditation is to relax into the natural or given openness of the dharmakaya, the more you become used to doing that, the more you can do it at any time or in any place since it is always there as the basis of everything that you are experiencing. It is always integrated with whatever is occurring. It is not so much about actively remembering as not doing the activity of forgetting.

Forgetting and ignoring are activities. Practising distraction takes effort. We are so used to making that effort that it has become automatic, normal, and seems natural. However once we relax we start to realise how much effort goes into maintaining the importance we invest in the structures of our life. We are all quite committed to the project of our individual life. We want our plans to be fulfilled, but life happens and we become disappointed.

The issue here is not about avoiding making plans, it is about the relation we have to the plan. The more we see the emptiness, the less we do this egocentric investment. This opens the space for compassion, for the thought of the other. The orientation of the bodhisattva is for the other. Instead of putting yourself into the task, you can put the other into the task. The more we are attentive to the other, the more we look at the task in terms of its utility and so we can modify the task to fit the other which means less attachment to the form of the task. At work this can mean less conflict with colleagues!

Maintaining this openness without needing to do formal meditation is our goal. As beginners, in order to get the taste of the space, we have to practise in a fairly formal way, but Nuden Dorje is advising us not to let the method make the experience artificial. Meditation should be as ordinary as breathing.

When we go outside there is space and people are moving about in the space. We walk, the birds fly, sounds arise, the wind blows on our face. This is the flow of experience, flowing because there is space for it to flow. The space of the mind is here, so relax out of any idea that 'I am walking' and just allow walking to occur in space. This is called 'meditating sky to sky'. The sky or the openness of the mind encounters the openness of the world. In the space of the world cars and horses move, and in the space of the mind thoughts, feelings and sensations move. These movements never stop. This is the inseparability of these two spaces – their non-duality – this is the non-duality of subject and other, or self and other.

'Remain free of encouraging or inhibiting, stability or movement.' Just allow t to happen. If you set a kind of benchmark or goal you create an idea of how the mind should be and this will bring you into developing and encouraging or inhibiting. This is not necessary because how it is, is how it is. Bad things happen and you feel sad. We can't stop bad things happening and we don't have to stop ourselves from being sad. These are movements in space so integrate the experience with space.

Verse 30: The Chain of Thoughts

'At the time of arising thoughts support each other like a chain of friends. At the time of dissolving they dissolve evenly in the vastness of openness. The ultimate nature of all phenomena is simply this.'

When we sit to practice thoughts keep coming and building up some very tempting pictures in our mind, pulling us in, and then they are gone. All of this stuff – and then it's gone. We began this weekend of teaching and practice by doing some calming shamatha practice. We focus on our breath and then we find we are distracted. We are caught by thoughts that vanish. A thought that seemed so powerful and real that we just went off with it, has now gone and it can't come back – it won't come back. That is what he is saying.

At first this thought is like a friend. The thought arises and puts its arm around you, *'Hey, let's have a little walk.'* Off you toddle together, and the minute you turn your head it's gone. *'Shit! What am I doing here? Back to my breath.'* This is what happens. It is not because you are bad or stupid or you don't know how to meditate. It is just the phenomenology of existence.

We see it is like this, and seeing what thoughts are like gives us more sense of whether to go with the thought or not. In tasting the openness of your mind you don't need the thought. In seeing the situation of the world you may follow the thought, for the other. All phenomena are generated out of thoughts which seem real and vanish; seeing the seeming-ness of the reality allows us to be less involved.

Now we are coming to the end of this teaching retreat and it can be interesting to observe how it feels to be getting ready to leave. There is a different feeling in the room. At first we were arriving, then we were in it, and now we are going out. We are here, but already going, and this is true of everything in life. Nothing is stable. The one simple practice that we can always do is to observe impermanence: morning, midday, afternoon and evening. Time never stops.

It may appear to us that time is a commodity, which is how it feels when we are alienated. Actually, we *are* time; it's not something we *have* but we are. Here... and here... and here. If we are here this is it, but when we go off in our mind going somewhere else we are not here, but we are also not *there*. When we are here there is enough time because this is how it is. *'Ah! But it shouldn't be this way.'* Once you start judging how things are you are already out of time. Working with circumstances and collaborating means being in time as it is.

THE SAFEST PLACE

Being in time – being here and now – is the safest place to be. Having thoughts of being somewhere else, with other people, in other times, may be enjoyable but we have to see that it brings much less advantage then actually being relaxed and open, being here and now, wherever we are.

Here is an example about not being in time, about not being here. A party of six men had set out to climb Mount Everest. Of course it takes a lot of energy and money to organise such a group and people invest a lot of importance in it. There is a basic rule that if you plan to reach the top you have to head back down by two o'clock, because when the sun goes down the wind and cold intensify. This group of experienced climbers were almost at the top but it was a day when the going had been very slow. Someone in the camp below was observing them with a telescope. He noticed it was after two o'clock but they kept going on, determined to reach the summit. A storm came up and they died. This is a strong example of what can happen when you have an idea that dislocates you from your actual situation.

This wonderful idea is wrapping you in a bubble of a mental world, but not the actual world, and then accidents happen.

Verse 31: Illusion and Ethics

'Don't pursue the deceitful phenomena which appear through the six senses. During the day or night, whatever activity you engage in, the notion of a doer and a deed is just a confusing illusion, like a dream or magic.'

Regarding the six senses, the most dangerous one is consciousness. The buddhist tradition describes five sense organs each of which has its own consciousness. There is also mental consciousness which takes the information coming through the senses and organises it into a pattern. This is the main site of self-deception. *'Come on! Let's keep going, I am sure we can get to the summit.'* When you have a strong idea like that it bends what you see and hear. The physical senses are saying, *Eh, hang on a minute, what is this?'* But the mind is saying it will be fine. You can end up pushing through without listening or seeing.

Nuden Dorje is advising us to be aware of how we mislead ourselves. Of course we can be too sensitive and that can lead to us feeling that everything is impossible, but we can also be too insensitive and keep pushing. We need to find the right point, and you cannot find this point in a book. It is not established by any map. Each of us has to know moment by moment whether to go forward or back. There are consequences either way. At the time of the Twin Towers collapsing in America many firemen and policemen died trying to help others. Clearly it was a very strange and terrifying event and the desire to do everything to help takes people over until they lose the clarity that something is not safe for them to do. *'I have to help — but it's not safe.'* What do you trust? Every year you can read about parents drowning trying to save their children in the water. We understand why, because in their desire to help the other they forget themselves, and they don't pay attention to the circumstances.

We can focus too much on the other, and we can focus too much on the self.

Nuden Dorje is talking here about this unified field of experience in which self and other always arise together. Staying with the fullest picture of this is when it's safest for us because we have the optimal reception of the necessary facts coming in through the senses.

'During the day or night, whatever activity you engage in, the notion of a doer and a deed is just a confusing illusion, like a dream or magic.'

We are participants in the emergent field of experience. When we separate ourselves out the world falls into different bits. When we are participating with the interactive field life is flowing through us as if we were dancing or singing in a group of people. If you are with the rhythm, if you are on the beat, if you are in the tune, it is a wonderful experience. This is what athletes refer to as 'being in the zone', and this is the possibility for us all the time – to be here. But once we start thinking of a doer – me – I am the one who is doing so, what am I doing? Then when you come into evaluation and thought and judgement you lose the beat.

VERSE 32: AWARENESS, AWARENESS, AWARENESS

'Don't try to block appearances; they are devoid of substantial reality. Towards whatever arises maintain an attitude free of limitation, without judgement or prejudice. At all times and in all situations maintain the state of alert awareness.'

This is why it is important from time to time to watch terrible programmes on television. You are watching something and you think you can't bear it. Relax into the out-breath and offer yourself to this terrible performance and feel the irritation. Thoughts are coming. *'How can they show this? How could they make such a programme?'* These are just thoughts. Relax into the breath – it's not going to kill you – it could even be helpful to you since it is showing how narrow you've become. Allowing exposure to what you don't like can be a practice that allows you to observe your own resistance and judgement. You don't have to live your life that way. It is not about forcing yourself to do things you don't want to do, but from time to time just observe how complacent and tight this circle of 'what I like' can become.

Making similar little experiments, doing things that make you uncomfortable, can be quite useful. For example, some people avoid eating in a restaurant on their own. They feel embarrassed and uncomfortable wondering what other people might think about them. If you are like that then this can be a useful little experiment to do. For meditators this kind of experience is really helpful. It is like a stick stirring the bottom of a pond and all the old leaves and bugs come to the surface, and then we see what we are frightened of. We might notice that other people are doing these things and it doesn't seem to bother them, so that is probably a sign that it's not going to kill us, but we still have this fear. So relax and breathe. Observe how your thoughts operate. When we believe in the thought we shrink ourselves; when we observe the thought we see that it passes by and the walls of the prison get thinner and thinner. Here the text is saying that appearances are devoid of substantial reality. The limit is not the thing in the world; it's ourselves.

I remember going once to a beautiful open air swimming pool and climbing up the ladder to go on the high diving board. I walked to the end and looked down. I took a deep breath, and walked back, giving myself a little pep talk. I went towards the end of the board again, looked again – not breathing – walked back and climbed down the ladder! On one level this is not a great experience, but these things are also very helpful. *'In this James body this is not for me. I don't come together in the way of being able to do that.'* All kinds of judgements about ourselves can arise at that point — that we have failed — that we should be braver, or whatever. This is just how it is — some doors open and some don't. You won't know unless you try. If you try and the door doesn't open, that is not a big mistake; it is just like a doctor palpating you to see where the pain is. By engaging with the world, you now know the actual shape of yourself rather than some idea.

RENOUNCING THE PLEASURE OF GOSSIP

'Towards whatever arises, maintain an attitude free of limitation, without judgement or prejudice.' Of course this is difficult to do because it means that you have to make a great renunciation. You have to renounce the joy of gossip because judgement means seeing what others are doing, and 'without judging' means 'it just is'. Judging is going out on to the world, and this is an activity that you don't need to do because it just is. People park their cars in the 'wrong' place. These things happen, so why are we surprised? It just is. We don't need to enter into judgements or evaluations or comments.

This means that you see what is there. It is not about some idealised vision. We see everything precisely and devoid of substance, but if judgement comes in then it is about 'some thing' and that depends on reification.

'At all times and in all situations maintain the state of alert awareness.' The Tibetan language has similar problems to our own languages, for example a verb, (maintain), is indicating doing something. In Verse 31 the text was telling us not to enter into **'the notion of a doer and a deed'**. So how do we maintain this? It is actually self-maintaining when we don't do distraction. The nature of the mind – the mind itself – means this is what is here; this is the given. It just is, so it is going to be there by itself. To maintain this sense is not like putting wood on a fire to keep it burning; rather it's maintained by avoiding distraction, or reification, or judgement, or by separating subject and object.

Verse 33: The Lie of our Lives

'Don't relax your alert attention for even an instant. It is vital to maintain non-distraction, non-grasping, and non-avoidance.'

We have to understand this in the same way. Attention means that we are here with what is here; if we are here we are attentive. We maintain our attention by not following after something else. To maintain, or not to lose it, sounds like a command to be active, but we relax – we are here – and this is it.

We get distracted and distraction feels like the fate of the victim. *'It just happened to me. I didn't mean to...it's not my fault.'* But you got distracted and the attention went from here to there. You gave yourself to the thought. This is a giving. This is a doing. Such is the subtle self-deception that goes on in our minds. What is here just is, and getting distracted is not 'just is' — it's an activity. We abandon ourselves. The way to avoid doing this is not to try harder but just to relax and be here.

Again and again this is the central point. He is saying you will be successful by not doing the things that make you unsuccessful; success is in just being here. This is not hard because here is where we are. We are here. We are not anywhere else, we are here, so being here shouldn't be too difficult.

However we *imagine* we are somewhere else. We have a thought, *'Oh, where's the car? What do I have to do? Is there enough petrol?'* If there is not enough petrol you will see this when you get to the car. You turn on the engine and you look at the dials. You can't turn on the engine now while you are sitting in this room so the thought doesn't help. Attending to the car before you drive is helpful. When you are in the car you do the things that you need to do when you are in the car. You check the lights, the mirrors, the seat height and so on. If you are with the car, 'car-ness' will arrive.

'It is vital to maintain non-distraction, non-grasping, and non-avoidance.' What does this mean? It means not trying hard to do this. This goes against all the things we learned in school: *'If you don't try hard, you won't pass your exams.'* Cause and effect. If you don't open the book, what is in the book won't jump inside you. If you want the result you have to activate the causal factors. This makes sense in terms of our participation in the world, because we are trying to go from not knowing arithmetic to knowing arithmetic. We are transforming ourselves.

But here the text is saying that this buddha nature or this enlightened nature is already present in all beings. We can't make it and it can't be destroyed. We can't lose it nor can we find it, because it is not a thing. Holding all of that in mind we try to understand what he is saying. How do we maintain or protect non-distraction? What we have got is enough. Being distracted, we think that there is something else which is better than here, but here is what we have.

It is very simple. If you are content, satisfied and complete with what is here, this is dzogpa chenpo, or the 'great completion', so why would you be distracted? What would be better than this? If you give yourself to this it's enough. But if you go up in your helicopter comparing and contrasting this and that, then it's different, because there is me, there is this, and then there is that. Which one do I want? This is thought production. If you stay in the ego's situation — in consciousness — attending to objects outside of yourself, then you find yourself being distracted and grasping at some things and avoiding other things. The practice is not about struggling not to do these old habits; it's about relaxing into the place where old habits can't catch you. Our ordinary consciousness, our dualistic ego, is like one side of Velcro tape because as soon as Velcro encounters the other side it locks on.

The mind (*sem-nyid*) itself is not like Velcro; it is like a smooth ball with no corners, cracks, or hooks so there is nothing to catch hold of — open, relaxed, contented. Nothing is missing so where would we go looking for more?

Nuden Dorje repeats the same points again and again. In fact the whole of dzogchen could be written on the back of an envelope. It is very simple, but it is difficult for us because we are complicated.

Verse 34: Be Kind to Yourself

'*Maintain emptiness and compassion without distraction or striving meditation. Always free of effort and struggle, contemplate the flow of meditative evenness and its subsequent effect.*' This verse is saying that if we rest in this open state we won't get distracted.

—Why not?

—Because distraction comes from abandoning our own ground.

—How do we abandon our own ground?

—By forgetfulness, which is linked with ignorance. We get caught up.

—Who is the one who gets caught up?

—I, me, myself.

—What is 'I, me, myself'?

—A patterning of mental arisings.

—What is the ground of these mental arisings?

—The ever-pure, ever-open mind itself.

Thoughts coming from the ground catch other thoughts and create the illusion, and in that decontextualisation there is a forgetfulness. It is just like that.

For example, somebody on your train gets a call on their mobile phone and they start to talk very loudly, generously sharing the nonsense of their life with everyone else on the train. Where are they? In their own little world. But that 'little world' is also in the train so people like me have to get up and say, '*Excuse me. You are talking very loudly.*' And they look at me as if I am so rude to be interrupting their private conversation! This is decontextualisation. They have lost the sense that they are sharing the space with other people because of the intoxication of this private world — but it is not private, it is public.

Again and again if you are here, you won't get lost. You can say,

—I am on the train and I can't talk now.

—But you have a phone. You can talk to me.

—But I am on a train so this is not the time to do it.

One very important notion in life is just because I **can**, doesn't mean I **have to**.

Modern technology enables people to do lots of things that were completely unnecessary some years ago, so they have become a new necessity. But they are not necessary. You don't have to have a mobile phone. But how would people contact you then? They can write a letter – it will take longer– and perhaps by the time the letter arrives the problem will have been solved. But we are on constant alert – here I am – ready for action. Ridiculous. We are not an Accident & Emergency Department.

'Always free of effort and struggle contemplate the flow of meditative evenness.' Staying relaxed is important. A lot of things are not important.

Sometimes people say to me,

—Oh, but if you were away, how could we get in touch with you if one of your children got very sick?

—If they were on their own then maybe they would die, and if somebody was with them then probably they would get taken to the hospital.

—But what would happen? You wouldn't be there.

—Maybe I would be there in time for the funeral.

People think this is very bad. The world is full of cemeteries and we are all going to die some day, but we don't know when. I have three sons and if they die, they die. I will be sad, but I am not a doctor and I can't stop them dying. If they die without me being there then that is what happens; that is just how it is.

A sailor on a boat can't suddenly sail home if their children are sick. Sickness and death happen. I am not causing their death by not being there, but there is this idea that we should be able to react and respond immediately.

—*Yes, but I can be here and there.*

When you are talking on the phone you are not here and you are not there either. You are what is called 'distracted'. Understanding distraction is very important.

—*Oh, but they really want to tell me what is happening.*

They need to learn patience. Patience is a traditional virtue.

—*But I want to tell you today.*

—*You can't.*

—*But I want to.*

This is called the disappointment of not having developed an attitude of patience. These are things that were completely natural to our grandparents' generation, but modern children don't understand this and are on the phone all the time. This is a distraction. The attention span of children in school gets less and less, so upholding these traditional virtues is very important. To be free of effort and struggle also means not leaping into unnecessary arousal.

There is a story told about Milarepa. When he was old he was meditating in a retreat in the mountains, along with many other yogis. One of the younger yogis came to him and said, '*We are here meditating all the time, but don't we need to show some compassion and go down and help the people in the valley?*' Milarepa told him,

'Well, if you stay here for another three years doing your meditation and becoming clearer, do you imagine that when you go back down into the valley there will be nobody left?'

Verse 35: Nothing Better Than This

'This practice is the longing for the essential meaning of all the classes of tantra, the vital essence of the dharma. It is the supreme practice of all the buddhas. It is the sole secret exposition of the view, meditation and conduct.'

Nuden Dorje is nearing the end of this text, and since it has covered a lot of material some of which is hard to understand, so now he gives a little encouragement. This practice is enough, is what this verse is saying. Enough is enough. Of course there are many other things he could say, but if you have enough, then more is harmful.

Garab Dorje, the buddha who first taught this dzogchen teaching in the human dimension, expressed this in his famous THREE STATEMENTS. The first statement is to open to your mind itself and be in touch with how it is; the second is not to remain in doubt; and the third is to continue in this way.

The first statement means enter the practice with the instruction and release all the clinging and attachment, letting it go free by itself. The second statement, not remaining in doubt, means don't enter into judgement about it. If you allow yourself into the space, that is the way to find yourself, but if you stand on the outside judging, comparing, contrasting, and thinking you remain in the realm of your isolated ego. The third statement – to continue in this way – means you don't need anything else.

There is always more. You could take up Sufi dancing, which is not a bad thing to do, and then you probably start to read books about Sufi ideas — all very interesting and helpful if you want to teach comparative religion, but if you turn it into a path then it is difficult to keep these two paths running together. You would be like a beginner skier whose skis are drifting apart — quite a painful experience. Better to stay on this one path if you want to, trusting that it is enough. *'Oh, but maybe I should do this, or maybe that.'* There is nothing wrong with thinking this, but now you have two...five ...or ten dharmas. Which one will I do? A bit of each of them? There is nothing wrong with this where food is concerned, since we need to eat a wide range of things for a healthy balanced diet. But it is not so good for finding a deep way into being with yourself. The more practices you have the more you have to work out which one to do when. This brings you to comparing and contrasting, and this is a distraction.

With regard to Garab Dorje, the first of his statements is sometimes called a 'pointing out' instruction. I can point out where my nose is but I can't point out where my mind is. I can introduce somebody to somebody else, but I can't really introduce you to your mind, or introduce your mind to you. *'Ego, meet mind. Mind, meet ego. I hope you two get on well together.'*

We are studying this text together now but afterwards you have to go off and do the practice yourself. I am cut off from myself, by myself. My own thoughts create the web of illusion and if I stay within that web I won't find the ground of my being. This is the teaching. If it makes sense to you, you have to sit and make friends with yourself. Nobody can do it for you, because it is you.

If you are helping a child to ride a bicycle, the fact that you can ride a bicycle means that you can give them a bit of encouragement. When the child sits on the bicycle you can keep hold of them at first to help them not fall off, but then you let go and they have to find their own balance. You can't give them balance. Nobody can give balance to anybody else. This is the important thing: it is your mind and you find it because it's yours, and it is not a thing.

You can give a child an ice cream or new shoes but you can't give them their sense of balance; they have to find it whilst not knowing what it is. Yesterday I was looking at a little girl on a bicycle, and it seemed as though she had just discovered this because she was so excited. The sun was shining out of her face because she is going fast and her big sister is running behind. She is herself. That's what balance does. *'I can do it. This is me.'* This is the function of the meditation: to come into ourselves. Freedom. Nuden Dorje is saying in this verse that everything we need is contained in this instruction.

Verse 36: The proper way

'The fortunate ones with good karma must do this practice, then the good qualities of the stages and paths will develop and increase. This is the distillation of the essence of dzogchen. It will be a friend to the fortunate ones who come later.'

The stages and paths are described in the general mahayana teachings. He is saying that everything which you find described in other texts as the fruit of particular techniques and practices, is a natural ripening if you stay with the truth of this practice.

When he mentions that *'it will be the friend for those who come later'* he is referring to us. The lineage for this teaching is very short. It is a terma teaching and so it comes originally from Padmasambhava, in this case through his disciple, Khyeuchung Lotsawa, who was reincarnated many centuries later as Nuden Dorje. Nuden Dorje passed it to his disciple who gave it to Gonpo Wangyal, who passed it on to Tulku Tsullo, who passed it to C R Lama, who taught it to me.

Verse 37: Maintain the Lineage

'You protectors of the treasure doctrines must guard these doctrines well. You vow-keepers must protect these teachings as if they were your child. You will see the face of Samantabhadra, the primordial purity of your awareness.'

When Padmasambhava went to Tibet there were many local gods of the mountains, rivers, lands and so on. The local people made offerings to these gods. When the local gods saw that a buddhist temple was being built at Samye they became angry because some new rival had arrived. Padmasambhava, through his meditation, entered into relation with these local gods and showed them that their power should serve the dharma, and some of these local gods then became protectors particularly of these terma or treasure teachings.

Nowadays we seem to live in a dead world. If we walk through the forest at night we feel a bit afraid. We don't know the name of any local spirit who lives there. We don't know how to make them some offerings or how to communicate with them. The world is just stuff. When Tibetans are preparing to build a house or a stupa or a monastery, they first enter into conversation with the owner of the land. This is not somebody who holds the deeds in the notary's office; it is the spirit who inhabits the land. They say, *'I want to build something. I know it will cause some disturbance for you but please don't be offended.'* This may seem very old fashioned but it speaks of the world as dialogue. They seek permission, since for them this is not an empty land.

When the British first went to Australia they thought the land was completely empty. Yes, there were a few aborigines but they thought they could kill them off quite quickly and declare Australia as their land. It was the same in North America, killing off the native people and saying, *'Oh, they didn't have pieces of paper, so it wasn't theirs, anyway it's mine now.'* This is domination, control, and genocide. This is the very opposite of collaboration and of being respectful to the environment; of seeing that whatever we do will have some impact on what is already here.

If you walk in the Himalayas you can see little stupas in the buddhist regions, and the perfection of the place where they are located is amazing. It is as if the local people are masters of feng shui and find exactly the right place. You can see these photos of small monasteries in Tibet just nestled in the right place in a particular valley, because they are working with the aesthetic completion of the setting; not attacking or dominating or imposing.

It is the same with this text; we should be respectful of it. The idea that it has protectors means that the energy of the world is on the side of dharma, and if we collaborate with dharma then this energy is on our side too. It is not about violence and domination, but the sense that there is enough space for everyone. We say that we want Ekajati, the main protector of the dzogchen teachings and many others, to be our friends and supporters.

VERSE 38: TEACHING FOR THE HEART AND NOT THE INTELLECT

'It is never appropriate to show these teachings to scholars who are addicted to ratiocination and point-scoring. They are sealed in emptiness. Because they are very secret, they are known as the dakinis' secret treasure.'

This verse says not to share this with scholars who use information as a means to an end, to develop a reputation, and to point out the faults of others. This text is an end in itself; it is complete and it is a way of encouraging us to come into the completion of ourselves. If we use this text to criticise other methods of meditation and practice then this is not helpful.

The world is a big place and there are many different kinds of people; some things take our fancy and some don't. What the text has been saying all the way through is to soften the idea that we have of self-existing real objects.

Some people will say that dzogchen is the highest teaching of all, but this is a statement of hostility to other paths. Dzogchen is the highest path for those who can make use of dzogchen. If it's not your cup of tea then it is not the highest teaching for you. It's not about the object, and it's not even about the subject; it's about the non-duality of subject and object.

In Tibetan culture they talk about things being your share – your *cha* – it means what is yours in this world, your luck.

I have a friend whose *cha* is horses. My mother also liked and rode horses. I don't like horses, so I have nothing to say to horses. I like talking to cows but I don't really like patting horses and giving them carrots, so it is not my share, my *cha*.

When we look at the world we each have things which shine for us and other things we don't get. We don't want to do violence by contorting ourselves to adopt a pattern or a path which is not for us. There are many dharma paths. We all know the story of Cinderella. In the end she is happy because the shoe and foot are a perfect fit, but for her two step-sisters it was a different story. One of them even cuts off her toe to force her foot in the shoe. *'But I really want it!'* But no, it is not for you.

Do the practice – open to it – and if it is your way you will find your way in it. You don't need to say that this is better than that, and explain how it fits into the whole pattern of buddhism. You may know some things about that but it can really get in the way of your practice.

This text belongs to a particular group of texts called THE DAKINIS' SECRET TREASURE (ZAB THIG MKHA' 'GRO'I GSANG MDZOD)

That is the end of the text but there is a brief colophon.

Verses 39 and 40: Colophon

'It is hidden for the fortunate one known as Bendza Ming.'

'Ming' means name, so it really means 'For the one known as Vajra'. 'Vajra' refers to Nuden Dorje who discovered the text.

'This text was revealed by Nuden Dorje Drophan Lingpa at the holy place of Kang Zang (Gangs bZang) in North Tibet. It was written down at Machig Labdron's pilgrimage place by Zangri Khamar [Zangs Ri mKhar dMar].'

After he wrote it down, he started to teach it to a few people. Now we have this text and now you have the explanation, so it is up to you whether you do the practice or not. You may put aside a weekend when you can study it and do more practice yourself; and you can also practise it in short periods, as we have described.

Sitting

Now we will do a final sitting through the Three 'A' practice.

Dedication

We share whatever merit arises from our study and practice together with all sentient beings. You can imagine rays of rainbow light spreading out from your heart in all directions to all beings.

Dedication of Merit

>GE WA DI YI NYUR DU DAG
>
>OR GYAN LA MA DRUB GYUR NAE
>
>DRO WA CHIG KYANG MA LU PA
>
>DE YI SA LA GO PAR SHO

By this virtue may I quickly attain the glorious Guru's stage.

Then may I put all beings without even one exception, on that same stage!

Our brief time together has come to an end and I am very grateful for the invitation to come here. I have enjoyed myself very much. Everything flows very easily together, so that is lovely for me.

Of course many people have been involved in organising and making sure that things work well and we have great gratitude to them. The mood of our meeting is generated by everyone's participation.

This dzogchen understanding may be quite difficult to find a way into at first. It may seem very abstract and intellectual. It is, in fact, about being present, moment-by-moment. For me, trying to offer this understanding to you, is deeply aided by the free attention that you give to it and I am very touched by the way people participate even when it is hard.

www.ingramcontent.com/pod-product-compliance
Lightning Source LLC
Chambersburg PA
CBHW070842160426
43192CB00012B/2273